Monitoring Indicators of the Visitor Experience and Resource Conditions in the Denali Backcountry

Summer 2010

Natural Resource Technical Report NPS/DENA/NRTR—2011/480

Peter J Fix

Department of Resources Management
School of Natural Resources and Agricultural Sciences
University of Alaska Fairbanks
Fairbanks, AK 99775-7200

Heidi Hatcher

Department of Resources Management
School of Natural Resources and Agricultural Sciences
University of Alaska Fairbanks
Fairbanks, AK 99775-7200

August 2011

U.S. Department of the Interior
National Park Service
Natural Resource Stewardship and Science
Fort Collins, Colorado

The National Park Service, Natural Resource Stewardship and Science office in Fort Collins, Colorado publishes a range of reports that address natural resource topics of interest and applicability to a broad audience in the National Park Service and others in natural resource management, including scientists, conservation and environmental constituencies, and the public.

The Natural Resource Technical Report Series is used to disseminate results of scientific studies in the physical, biological, and social sciences for both the advancement of science and the achievement of the National Park Service mission. The series provides contributors with a forum for displaying comprehensive data that are often deleted from journals because of page limitations.

All manuscripts in the series receive the appropriate level of peer review to ensure that the information is scientifically credible, technically accurate, appropriately written for the intended audience, and designed and published in a professional manner. This report received formal, high-level peer review based on the importance of its content, or its potentially controversial or precedent-setting nature. Peer review was conducted by highly qualified individuals with subject area technical expertise and was overseen by a peer review manager.

This report is available from the Murie Science and Learning Center, Denali National Park and Preserve (http://www.murieslc.org/) and the Natural Resource Publications Management website (http://www.nature.nps.gov/publications/nrpm/).

Please cite this publication as:

Fix, P. J. and H. Hatcher. 2011. Monitoring indicators of the visitor experience and resource conditions in the Denali backcountry: Summer 2010. Natural Resource Technical Report NPS/DENA/NRTR—2011/480. National Park Service, Fort Collins, Colorado.

NPS 184/109205, August 2011

Table of Contents

Figures

Tables

Tables (continued)

Tables (continued)

Tables (continued)

Tables (continued)

Abstract

The Denali Backcountry Management Plan specifies indicators of resource conditions and the visitor experience. This study developed a visitor survey to measure the level of the indicators experienced by the visitors. Both overnight backpackers and day hikers were included in the sample; different surveys were developed for the two groups. Completed surveys were received from 191 backpackers (42% response rate) and 446 day hikers (77.4% response rate). A non-response test did not reveal differences that would bias results. Comparisons of the indicators to the standards were conducted three ways: 1) comparing the mean level, or percent when appropriate, of the indicators to the standard, 2) estimating for how many individuals the standard was violated, and 3) calculating the number of days in which the standard was violated for at least one individual. Results indicate that overall, for both backpackers and day hikers, the indicators of natural sound disturbance and encounters with modern equipment had mean levels above the standard of one and zero, respectively, with 59.8% of backpackers and 51.8% of day hikers reporting a level of motorized sound above the standard and 27.1% of backpackers and 45.4% of day hikes reporting a level of encounters with modern equipment above the standard. In addition, both groups had a higher percent seeing litter or human waste than the standard of five percent; 11.2% and 14.1% for backpackers and day hikers, respectively. For backpackers the mean level of landscape modifications was not statistically different than the standard, and the level of encounters with other park visitors, groups larger than six, and NPS rangers or researchers was below the standard. On seven percent of nights camped, backpackers were unable to camp out of sight or sound of others. For day hikers, the mean level of encounters with other parties was above the standard of two per day, with 48.2% of respondents reporting levels above two. Overall, on average, day hikers did not violate the standards for encounters with large groups (>6 people) or NPS rangers or researchers. Analysis of backpacker response data by backcountry unit found that the motorized sound and landscape modification standards were violated by at least one individual of most all units of the backcountry; 27 and 28 units, respectively, of the 32 units in which respondents hiked revealed some level of standard violation for the two indicators mentioned. For the indicators of litter and human waste, modern equipment, and encounters with others, 10, 11, and 20 units out of the 32, respectively, did *not* violate the standard. Examining day hiker data with the criterion that a unit's standard is violated if any one person in that unit encounters a condition above the standard shows for the indicators of motorized sound, landscape modifications, encounters with modern equipment, and encounters with other parks visitors there were very few backcountry units that met existing standards when using this strict interpretation of violation; one, one, four, and four units, respectively, of the 28 units in which respondents day hiked, were entirely within standard. Twenty units violated the litter and human waste standard and 8 units violated the large group standard. For results presented by unit it should be cautioned that some units had few respondents that hiked in them, reducing the representation of all hikers within those units.

Acknowledgements

Matthew Helt assisted in conducting a pretest of the survey instrument in the summer of 2008. Leah Roach was the lead for gathering the data during the summer of 2010, including conducting interviews. Leah also entered the data and transcribed the interviews. Courtney Mitchell assisted Leah in gathering the data. The staff at the Backcountry Information Center distributed the survey to the overnight backpackers. Adrienne Lindholm was the initial lead on the project for the National Park Service, and contributed to the study design and survey development. Jessica Toubman, Backcountry Desk Supervisor, provided reviews of several drafts of the survey, provided information on characteristics of backpackers, and relayed information regarding the study to her staff. Andrew Ackerman, Social Scientist in Denali National Park and Preserve, took over as project lead and provided valuable help with project logistics. Lucy Tyrrell, Research Administrator Denali National Park and Preserve, assisted with permitting of the project, arranging housing, and other project logistics. Joe Fix assisted with formatting; Nancy Tarnai assisted with editing.

Introduction

The Denali National Park and Preserve Back Country Management Plan (BCMP), which was adopted in 2006 (National Park Service 2006), is based on the Visitor Experience and Resource Protection (VERP) management framework (National Park Service 2005). Key steps of VERP, and all other recreation management frameworks, are to identify indictors of resource and experiential condition and selection of standards for each of the indicators that are targeted at meeting desired conditions for specific management areas. The BCMP defines indicators as specific, measurable physical, ecological, or social variables that reflect the overall condition of an area. Standards are the minimum acceptable condition for each indicator variable. The planning process for the BCMP resulted in six indicators of resource conditions and five indicators of social conditions.

The indicators of *resource conditions*, as listed on page 35 in the plan, are:
- Trail and campsite disturbance
- Evidence of modern human use (referred to as "modern equipment" in this report)
- Landscape modifications
- Litter and human waste
- Natural sound disturbance (referred to as "motorized sound" in this report)
- Wildlife population, demographics and distribution (will not be discussed in this report)

The indicators of *social conditions* are:
- Encounters with people (referred to as "other park visitors" in this report)
- Encounters with large groups
- Camping density (referred to as "camp out of sight or sound" in this report)
- Accessibility
- Administrative presence

Definitions of the Denali National Park and Preserve BCMP indicators

Definitions of the indicators as taken from "Table 2: Key to Management Area Descriptions" on page 33 of the BCMP Summary (National Park Service, n.d.) are as follows.

Evidence of modern human use

Modern equipment includes communication facilities, research equipment, chain saws, motorized or mechanized vehicles on the ground, and other similar devices. This definition does not include portable devices that a person could reasonably carry without assistance (e.g., cell phones, GPS units, fuel-burning stoves), subsistence equipment such as traps or firearms, or aircraft in flight. An "encounter" refers to visual recognition. A single trail or route markers associated with a single route will count as only one encounter. Audio recognition of noise is covered under the Natural Sound Disturbance standard.

Landscape Modifications

Landscape modification include visible mitigations for visitor use such as constructed trail segments, route markers, signs, bridges, designated campsites, food storage facilities, sanitation facilities, and fixed climbing lines. Landscape modifications specifically do not include historic or cultural resources such as historic cabins, gravesites, or other structures or artifacts. They also do not include permitted modifications for subsistence use such as cabins or trapline trails.

Natural Sound Disturbance

"Audible" means audibility to a person of normal hearing. Maximum sound levels assume the measurement device is more than 50 feet from the noise source.

Encounters with People

An encounter is the unaided recognition by sight or sound of another park user, including other recreationalists or subsistence users. An encounter does not include aircraft in flight which are addressed under Natural Sound Disturbance.

Camping Density

This category refers only to the opportunity to camp outside of sight or sound of other park visitors; however, visitors may still choose to camp where they can see or hear others. "Sight or sound" refers to unaided recognition of another campsite from the site where the visitor camps for the night.

Administrative Presence

This category only includes interactions with administrative and research personnel, which are not included in Encounters with People. Interactions with park aircraft, research equipment, snowmachines, or other equipment are included in the standards for Evidence of Modern Human Use and Natural Sound Disturbance.

Management Areas and Standards

The BCMP divides the backcountry into six management areas (A, B, C, D, OP1, and OP2), in addition to special use area overlays (e.g., Portal, Corridor, Ruth Glacier Special Use). Each management area and special use area have different standards; the different standards define the management area and shape the resource conditions and experience the visitor can expect in the area. The management areas and the associated standards are shown in Appendix A. More detailed information regarding the management areas and standards can be found in the BCMP.

Study Objectives

The BCMP specifies that monitoring of the indicators, with the exception of trail and campsite disturbance and accessibility, would be conducted *at least once every five years by visitor survey*. The plan also states that the first visitor survey after plan approval would contain questions to evaluate the usefulness of the evidence of modern human use indicator and investigate other alternatives for indicating the impact of modern civilization on the wilderness experience.

This study was the first measure of the indicators after the BCMP was adopted. The objectives of the study were to 1) survey a representative sample of backcountry visitors accessing areas of the park via the Denali Park Road to assess the level of the indicators they experienced, 2) quantify results in multiple ways (e.g., by unit, by day), and 3) compare the levels of the indicators as measured by the survey to the standards. A secondary goal was to gather information on the relative importance of a lack of evidence of modern human use on the backcountry visitor experience and explore alternative ways to measure or determine at what levels influence of modern society negatively impacts the Denali backcountry experience.

Methods

Survey Design

The initial survey was designed with staff from the planning division in the Anchorage Regional Office. The survey was designed to gather the required information while keeping the length as short as possible. For indicators that were to be compared to a standard that expressed a numeric value (i.e., evidence of modern human use, landscape modifications, natural sound disturbance, encounters with people, encounters with large groups, and administrative presence), questions were developed to ask respondents how often they encountered the indicators. The standards for litter and human waste and for camping density are expressed as a percent of visitors who encounter the condition and do not take into consideration the frequency of the encounter (i.e., less than 5% of visitors encounter litter or human waste; backpacker should always be able to camp out of sight or sound of others). Questions for these two indicators were formatted as polar Yes/No questions and asked respondents if they saw litter, toilet paper, and/or human waste and if they were able to camp out of sight or sound of others. For evidence of modern human use, landscape modifications, natural sound disturbance, and encounters with others respondents were asked what percent of time the indicator was present. To assess the importance of the different indicators a set of questions was developed that asked the respondents to rate the importance of encountering a low level of modern human use; landscape modifications; natural sound disturbance; encounters with other visitors; large groups; and litter, toilet paper and/or human waste.

The above questions were common in the surveys provided to both the day hiker and backpacker . The day hiker survey was printed on both sides of an 8 ½ x 11" sheet of paper, and also asked respondents what units they hiked in, whether they hiked on an established trail, and how long they hiked. A map was provided on the front of the survey. The backpacker survey was a booklet consisting of several pages in which the questions repeated. Respondents were instructed to complete a separate page for each day of their hike, or if they hiked in more than one unit in a day, each unit in which they hiked.

A pilot test of the survey was conducted in summer of 2008, revisions to the survey were made and the survey was submitted to the United States Office of Management and Budget (OMB) for approval. OMB approval was granted in late summer 2009.

Prior to the summer 2010 field season, several additions to the study design and survey were made. First days hikers were asked if they hiked farther than ½ mile from the park road. If yes, they were instructed to complete the survey only for the indicators they experienced while farther than ½ mile from the road. This change was made to determine if impacts were significantly higher in backcountry areas that are in close proximity to the road. Second, the survey administrator would provide the responding day hikers with a map of the unit in which they hiked, printed on 8 ½ x 11" paper, and ask them to draw their route. Third, backpackers were asked to draw their route on a map that was included on the cover of the survey. Fourth, based on feedback from NPS staff that the question asking respondents to "rate the importance of a low level of the conditions specified by the indicators" was confusing, the question was changed to ask respondents to rate the level of impact on their backcountry experience when encountering these conditions.

The final surveys are shown in Appendix B.

Sampling

A pilot test conducted in the summer of 2008 tested methods of sampling day hikers before they boarded the bus (having them take the survey and return it after their hike) and after their hike. The percentage of people agreeing to take the survey was slightly higher pre-hike (91% vs. 81%), however, a low percent of the pre-hike surveys was completed and returned (30%); in contrast 85% of those who agreed to complete the survey post-hike returned a completed survey. It was determined sampling day hikers post-hike is the preferred method.

The day hikers were sampled at three locations: the Wilderness Access Center (WAC), the Savage River parking area and the Triple Lakes trailhead. As variance of survey responses was expected to be low at Savage River and Triple Lakes, 92% of the sampling effort was at the WAC.

To sample day hikers who rode a bus, we sampled at the WAC when buses returned. Sampling occurred between June 1 and September 5, a 97 day span. Each day was split into early afternoon (from 1:30 to 6:30 p.m.) and evening (from 6:30 to 10:30 p.m.) time blocks, for 194 possible time blocks to sample. Seventy-two time blocks to sample visitors at the WAC were randomly selected. In addition, three blocks each were selected to sample at Savage River parking area and Triple Lakes trailhead. See Appendix C for a list of the time blocks selected for sampling.

When passengers departed the bus they were asked if they had hiked in the backcountry. Visitors who had hiked were asked if they would be willing to complete the survey. Those agreeing were asked what unit they hiked in, and a map of that unit was provided along with the survey. The respondent was asked to draw their route on the map. At the Savage River parking area and Triple Lakes trailhead, visitors were asked if they would be willing to complete the survey as they returned from their hike.

The majority of backpackers were sampled at the Backcountry Information Center (BIC). Sampling occurred from June 1 to September 5, a 97 day span. Days were split into morning (9 a.m. to 1:30 p.m.) and afternoon time blocks (1:30 to 5 p.m.), and 71 time blocks were randomly selected. As an informal test of the effect of administering the survey before the hike vs. after the hike, backpackers were sampled as they returned on the camper bus. However, there was not a formal, randomized schedule for the backpacker post-hike sample.

Non Response Test

A concern with survey research is that those who do not respond to the survey are different than those who do. Significant differences could bias the results. To test for this potential bias, information must be gathered on non-respondents. For day hikers we asked those who did not complete the survey two questions from the survey (how often they encountered motorized noise and how many groups they encountered while hiking), their age, and zip code of their home residence. In addition we observed and recorded their group size and gender. For backpackers, it was not feasible to ask additional questions of non-respondents, however, group size, length of trip, gender and residency were recorded on the backcountry permit and that information was used for a non-response test.

4

Analysis

The survey questions resulted in data at different "measurement levels" (Table 1). Means were reported for variables with continuous data, and t-tests and Analysis of Variance (ANOVA) were used when comparisons were appropriate. Frequencies were reported for variables with categorical and dichotomous data, and the Chi-square test was used when comparisons were appropriate (Vaske, 2008). Length of trip and group size were collapsed to categorical data in several instances with the appropriate analysis conducted. The 95% confidence intervals around the mean, or the percentage, are included in tables showing analysis by unit. Confidence intervals were included when they could be calculated, however, many of the units have low ns and, thus, very wide confidence intervals. While it is unusual to report confidence intervals with such low ns (as low as two in some cases), they were included to serve as a warning not to generalize the data from those units beyond the sample.

Table 1. Level of Measurement of Variables from Survey Questions.

Questions	Measurement level of variables
Report the level of the indicator, group size, length of trip	Continuous
Percent of time encountering the indicators, zip code	Categorical
Gender, encounters with litter/waste, camping out of sight/sound	Dichotomous

The purpose of measuring the indicators is to compare their level to the standards set in the BCMP. The BCMP contains 6 management areas, in addition to special use area overlays, with differing standards. All but two of the backcountry units utilized by respondents of this study were in the "Old Park 1" (OP1) management area. The standards for the OP1 management area are shown in Table 2. Units 41 and 42, which were utilized by several backpackers, are in management area "B". There are two differences between the "OP1" area standards and the "B" area standards: 1) the motorized sound encounter standard in area "B" is 10 per day and audible up to 15% of an hour, and 2) there is to be a "low" level of encounters (occasional patrols) with NPS rangers or researchers.

Table 2. Level of the Standard for Each Indicator in "OP1" Management Area.

Indicator	Standard
Encounters with motorized sound	No more than one per day, audible less than 5% of any hour
Encounters with modern equipment[1]	No more than one per day
Encounters with landscape modifications	No landscape modifications are visible
Encounters with other park visitors	No more than two per day
Encounters with groups > 6	One or two per day[2]
Encounters with NPS rangers or researchers	"Medium" (routine patrols)
Encounters with litter and human waste	Less than 5% reporting
Ability to camp out of sight or sound of others	Always

[1]As defined in "Table 1: Management Area Descriptions" in the BCMP summary (National Park Service n.d.), which lists the standard as "low 1 encounter/day." This differs from "Table 2. Key to the Management Area Descriptors" in the BCMP summary which lists the standard for low as no more than 1 encounter per trip. No more than one per day will be used throughout this report.
[2]As stated in the BCMP. However, in this report two will be used as the standard.

There are several ways in which the indicators can be reported and compared to the standards.

1. The mean level of the indicators can be computed and compared to the standards.

5

- This is the least conservative comparison, as the standard could be significantly violated for individuals without the overall level being exceeded.
2. A "zero tolerance," i.e., if one person violates the standard, the standard is considered to be violated.
   - This is the most conservative comparison.
   - This method could also be applied to a percentage of visitors (e.g., is the standard violated for five percent or more of visitors).
3. The number of days in which a standard is violated
   - Can be calculated for the mean level or zero tolerance.

For this report the mean levels are provided by unit and compared to the standards, the percent of respondents reporting levels of indicators above the standard and the percent of units violating the standards are reported, and the number of days in which the standard is violated under a zero tolerance scenario are reported. When results of means are presented, all units are reported, however discussion focuses only on those units with an $n >= 10$.

The importance of indicators was examined through content analysis of the interviews. The questions asking respondents to rate the impact encountering the conditions specified by the indicators has on their experience were misinterpreted by the respondents. Many answered whether the conditions did impact their experience, as noted by comments written next to the questions (e.g., "didn't encounter"), rather than if encountering the conditions would impact their experience if encountered. Because of this, the results from those questions are not presented.

Concerns Regarding Survey Design

Difference between Measured Level of Indicators and Conceptualization of the Standards: A critical note regarding a difference in the measured level of the indicators and the standards should guide comparison of the indicators to the standards. The initial conceptualization of the survey and the development of the questions that followed explicitly included impacts originating in the road corridor but visible in the backcountry. However, the standards include only impacts originating within the backcountry, i.e., they exclude impacts originating in the road corridor. Therefore, the level of the indicators might be overstated.

Different Interpretations of the Opportunity to Camp Out of Sight or Sound of Others: The survey asked respondents if they were able to camp out of sight and sounds of others. However, the indicator might intend "opportunity" to be the backpacker's first choice of campsite. As an example, consider the following situation. A backpacker has identified on a topographic map a spot on a distant ridge as the target for setting up camp, but upon arriving at the ridge she finds another party camped there and continues on to find a spot out of sight or sound of others. Interpreting "opportunity" as the backpacker's first choice of campsite, the standard (of always camping out of sight or sound) is violated. However, the survey would have measured that the backpacker did camp out of sight or sound of others.

Wording of the Landscape Modification Question: A concern was expressed midway through the sampling that visitors might be including animal trails as landscape modifications, i.e., they could not distinguish between human caused trails and animal trails. To test to see if this were occurring, the survey was changed so the description of landscape modifications explicitly included "constructed or human caused trails" and instructed respondents to "not include animal trails." The responses on the different versions of the survey were compared. In addition, a small number of respondents were asked how they interpreted the landscape modification question. Findings are presented in the results section.

Results

Response Rate

Backpackers at Backcountry Information Center
The contacts and completed surveys at the BIC are as follows:

- 365 hikers were contacted
- 26 refused to take the survey
- 186 did not refuse, but did not return the survey
- 153 surveys were completed (38 were completed post hike at the WAC, see section on next page)
- Response rate = 42%
- The resulting sample sizes for different observations of the indicators were 525 – 564 (Because not all questions were answered by all respondents, the range of observations (i.e., 525 – 564 across the indicators is provided.)

Table 3. Response Rate by Residency, Backpackers.

Residency	Response rate[1]
Local to Denali (zip 99755)	28%
Alaska non-local	39%
Lower 48	48%
International	45%

[1]The response rate shown is within each residency group.

Non-response Test Backpackers: To determine if those who responded to the survey differed from those who did not respond, the mean level, or percent within a category, of the following list of variables were compared between respondents and non-respondents by use of a t-test or chi-square test. The only significant difference was found for residency. The test statistics and *p* values are as follows:

- Group size ($t = -1.27, p = 0.21$)
- Length of trip ($t = 1.04, p = 0.30$)
- Gender ($\chi^2 = 0.08, p = 0.78$)
- Residency ($\chi^2 = 9.89, p = 0.02$)

As residency differed between respondents and non-respondents, indicators were compared by residency. Encounters with other park visitors differed (Table 4). To test if this resulted in non-response bias, data were weighted for residency and mean levels of the indicators were compared between weighted and unweighted data. Comparisons did not reveal differences that are of practical concern (Table 5). Backpacker data were not weighted for any of the analysis in this report.

Table 4. Mean Level of Indicators by Residency of Backpackers.

	Denali Local	Alaska Non-local	Lower 48	International
n[1]	59 – 62	43 – 47	264 – 274	50 – 54
Sound[2]	3.08	4.67	3.26	2.70
Modern equipment	1.05	1.76	1.05	1.22
Landscape modifications	1.43	1.15	1.02	0.98
Park visitors[2]*	0.50	1.14	0.69	0.96
Groups > 6	0.02	0.06	0.03	0.02

[1]Includes only the surveys administered at the BIC.
[2]Unequal variance, Welch statistic used.
* Significant at $p = 0.10$

Table 5. Overall Mean Level of Indicators by Data Weighted by Location of Residency vs. Not Weighted.

	Unweighted	Weighted
n[1]	435 – 453	410 – 428
Sound	3.43	3.33
Modern equipment	1.15	1.15
Landscape modifications	1.08	1.12
Other park visitors	0.75	0.73
Groups > 6	0.03	0.03

[1]Includes only the surveys administered at the BIC.

Backpacker Surveys Administered at the Wilderness Access Center

We sampled 41 backpackers, who were not sampled at the BIC, as they returned to the WAC on a camper bus. Thirty-eight completed a survey. Slight differences were found in the overall mean levels of motorized and modern equipment between the pre and post sample (Table 6). However, this does not necessarily reflect a bias in either of the sampling methods. First, the pre sample represented 82 different days of hiking; the post sample 52. There were 36 days represented by the pre sample but not by the post sample, and six days represented by the post sample but not the pre sample. Comparisons are difficult when the days are not the same. In addition, the units differ as the pre sample represented 32 units and the post sample 21 units (all of which were included in the pre sample). Comparing the indicators between the two samples by unit is difficult as many of the post hike units have low *n*s and thus low statistical power to detect differences. Nonetheless, comparing the 21 units on the level of motorized sounds reported, only unit 11 with an n of four, was statistically different. As differences in reported levels of the indicators appear to be due to different sample size or times sampled, the two samples were combined for the analysis of the indicators included in this report.

Table 6. Mean Level of Indicators, Backpacker Surveys Completed at the BIC and WAC.

	BIC (Pre)[1]	WAC (Post)[2]	t	p
Sound	3.44	2.18	2.72	0.007
Equipment	1.13	0.47	3.73	< 0.001
Landscape modifications	1.09	0.81	1.51	0.132
Other park visitors	0.75	0.83	-0.48	0.634
Groups > 6	0.03	0.06	-0.91	0.367
NPS Encounters	0.02	0.07	-1.82	0.071

[1]Data analyzed by days of the hike, ns ranged from 424 to 446.
[2]Data analyzed by days of the hike, ns ranged from 97 to 106.

For backpackers, surveys were administered in the morning and afternoon. It appears more people refused in the afternoon (65% vs. 52%). Rangers at the BIC observed that visitors getting their permit in the afternoon were more likely to be in a rush to catch a bus, and this contributed to their higher refusal rate. In addition, the locals, who had the lowest response rate, were slightly more likely to get their permit in the morning, further supporting that the time of day had an effect on response rate among all groups (i.e., overall, the time block offset the lower response rate of the locals).

Day Hikers at the Wilderness Access Center

The contacts and completed surveys for day hikers at the WAC are as follows:

- 576 day hikers were contacted
- 446 completed a survey
- Response rate = 77.4%

Non-response Tests Day Hikers: A key question is whether those who did not respond differed from those who did. To determine if there was a difference, the following variables were tested between respondents and non-respondents:

- Age
- Group size
- Motorized sound encounters
- Encounters with other park visitors
- Gender
- Residency

Of the comparisons between respondents and non-respondents, the only difference was that non-respondents had a smaller average group size than respondents (Table 7 – Table 8). To examine whether the difference in group size between respondents and nonrespondents might influence results, the level of the indicators were compared by group size; differences were found for several indicators (Table 9). Given that differences were found, data were weighted by group size categories of $1 - 3, 4 - 6, 7 - 10$, and 11+ and weighted and unweighted data were compared. No differences were found. Unweighted data were used for the day hiker analysis in this report.

Table 7. Non-response Test for Day Hikers, Continuous Variables.

	Respondents	Non-respondents	t	p
Age				
Mean	42.2	44.9	-1.66	0.097
N	440	92		
Std. dev.	14.3	15.2		
Group size				
Mean	3.9	3.0	3.55	< 0.001
N	442	122		
Std. dev.	3.1	2.2		
Motorized sound encounters				
Mean	3.2	2.1	1.20	0.233
N	388	45		
Std. dev.	5.7	3.7		
Encounters with other park visitors				
Mean	5.9	8.5	-1.60	0.115
N	394	46		
Std. dev.	10.6	12.5		

Table 8. Non-response Test for Day Hikers, Dichotomous and Categorical Variables.

	Respondents	Non-respondents	Pearson Chi-Square Tests Value	Asymp. Sig. (2-sided)
Gender (n=572)			0.12	0.732
Male	52.2%	54.0%		
Female	47.8%	46.0%		
Location (n=498)			2.79	0.425
Denali locals (zip = 99755)	4.6%	1.5%		
Other Alaskans	10.6%	12.3%		
Other USA	74.4%	70.8%		
International	10.4%	15.4%		

Table 9. Comparison of Indicators by Day Hiker Group Size.

	Groups of 3 or less	Groups of 4 or more	t	p
Motorized sound encounters				
Mean	3.6	2.2	2.78	0.006
N	259	170		
Std. Dev.	6.3	4.1		
Modern equipment encounters				
Mean	2.7	1.0	3.15	0.002
N	236	153		
Std. Dev.	8.1	1.6		
Landscape modifications				
Mean	2.4	1.3	2.75	0.006
N	231	149		
Std. Dev.	5.4	1.6		
Encounters w/other park visitors				
Mean	6.9	4.8	1.94	0.053
N	271	164		
Std. Dev.	11.7	8.6		
Encounters w/groups of size >6				
Mean	.7	.6	0.41	0.680
N	260	168		
Std. Dev.	2.1	1.6		
Encounters with NPS personnel				
Mean	.6	.6	-0.17	0.866
N	266	168		
Std. Dev.	1.3	.9		

Demographics

Data for the demographic variables were asked of all day hikers sampled and recorded for all backpackers, even if they did not complete the survey. The responses in this section reflect the entire sample of day hikers and the entire sample of backpackers from the BIC, not just those who completed the survey.

Table 10. Residency of Day Hikers and Backpackers.

Residency	Day hikers[1]	Backpackers[1]
Denali locals (zip = 99755)	4.4%	24.4%
AK not local to Denali	10.7%	15.7%
Other United States	73.8%	48.1%
Foreign	11.1%	11.7%

[1]The *n*s were 504 and 360 for day hikers and backpackers, respectively.

Table 11. Sex of Day Hikers and Backpackers.

Sex	Day Hikers[1]	Backpackers[1]
Male	52.8%	68.5%[c]
Female	47.2%	31.5%

[1]The *n*s were 579 and 359 for day hikers and backpackers, respectively.

Table 12. Age of Day Hikers[1].

Age Groups of Respondents	Day Hikers[2]
18 – 29 years of age	24.2%
30 – 39	21.8%
40 – 49	15.9%
50 – 59	22.3%
60 – 69	11.8%
70 and above	2.3%

[1]Question not asked to backpackers
[2]n=533, ages ranged from 18 to 73 years with a mean age of 42.2 years.

Characteristics of Hikes

Backpackers

Group Size of Backpackers: The distribution of group size was skewed to smaller group sizes (Table 13).

Table 13. Group size of Backpackers.

Group size	Backpackers (BIC)[1]	Backpackers (all)[1]
1	19.2%	22.1%
2	55.0%	53.8%
3	14.1%	12.9%
4	8.3%	8.2%
5	1.4%	1.5%
6 – 10	1.8%	1.5%
>10	-	-

[1]*n*s were 362, 403 for backpackers BIC (i.e., only those sampled at the BIC) and all (includes the post-hike sample), respectively. Includes respondents and non-respondents.

14

Units and Days of Backpackers' Hikes: Backpackers in the sample hiked in 32 different units (Table 14) on 88 different days (Table 15). The distribution of backpackers was not even throughout the summer.

Table 14. Units Hiked in by Backpackers in the Sample.

Unit	Frequency	%	Unit	Frequency	%
3	2	.4	24	3	.5
4	15	2.7	25	2	.4
5	19	3.4	26	18	3.2
6	63	11.2	28	5	.9
7	16	2.8	29	12	2.1
8	20	3.6	30	3	.5
9	48	8.5	31	27	4.8
10	52	9.3	32	34	6.0
11	15	2.7	33	31	5.5
12	38	6.8	34	23	4.1
13	35	6.2	35	9	1.6
14	1	.2	36	2	.4
15	7	1.1	38	3	.5
16	1	.2	39	16	2.8
18	24	4.3	41	3	.5
19	7	1.2	42	9	1.6

Table 15. Days[1] in which Indicator Data were Recorded by Backpackers.

Date	n	%	Date	n	%	Date	n	%
31-May-2010	1	0.2	01-Jul-2010	6	1.1	01-Aug-2010	3	0.5
01-Jun-2010	1	0.2	02-Jul-2010	11	1.9	02-Aug-2010	4	0.7
03-Jun-2010	1	0.2	03-Jul-2010	7	1.2	03-Aug-2010	6	1.1
04-Jun-2010	5	0.9	04-Jul-2010	5	0.9	04-Aug-2010	4	0.7
05-Jun-2010	4	0.7	05-Jul-2010	6	1.1	05-Aug-2010	5	0.9
06-Jun-2010	3	0.5	06-Jul-2010	7	1.2	06-Aug-2010	7	1.2
07-Jun-2010	2	0.4	07-Jul-2010	7	1.2	07-Aug-2010	13	2.3
08-Jun-2010	1	0.2	08-Jul-2010	9	1.6	08-Aug-2010	11	1.9
10-Jun-2010	3	0.5	09-Jul-2010	5	0.9	09-Aug-2010	8	1.4
11-Jun-2010	3	0.5	10-Jul-2010	8	1.4	10-Aug-2010	7	1.2
12-Jun-2010	3	0.5	11-Jul-2010	6	1.1	11-Aug-2010	10	1.8
13-Jun-2010	6	1.1	12-Jul-2010	10	1.8	12-Aug-2010	12	2.1
14-Jun-2010	4	0.7	13-Jul-2010	12	2.1	13-Aug-2010	10	1.8
15-Jun-2010	6	1.1	14-Jul-2010	7	1.2	14-Aug-2010	8	1.4
16-Jun-2010	3	0.5	15-Jul-2010	5	0.9	15-Aug-2010	5	0.9
17-Jun-2010	4	0.7	16-Jul-2010	5	0.9	16-Aug-2010	5	0.9
18-Jun-2010	5	0.9	17-Jul-2010	7	1.2	17-Aug-2010	2	0.4
19-Jun-2010	9	1.6	18-Jul-2010	11	1.9	18-Aug-2010	4	0.7
20-Jun-2010	9	1.6	19-Jul-2010	5	0.9	19-Aug-2010	4	0.7
21-Jun-2010	18	3.2	20-Jul-2010	9	1.6	20-Aug-2010	2	0.4
22-Jun-2010	13	2.3	21-Jul-2010	8	1.4	22-Aug-2010	2	0.4
23-Jun-2010	16	2.8	22-Jul-2010	7	1.2	23-Aug-2010	1	0.2
24-Jun-2010	15	2.7	23-Jul-2010	7	1.2	24-Aug-2010	2	0.4
25-Jun-2010	12	2.1	24-Jul-2010	5	0.9	25-Aug-2010	3	0.5
26-Jun-2010	7	1.2	25-Jul-2010	5	0.9	26-Aug-2010	4	0.7
27-Jun-2010	5	0.9	26-Jul-2010	4	0.7	27-Aug-2010	8	1.4
28-Jun-2010	11	1.9	27-Jul-2010	9	1.6	28-Aug-2010	8	1.4
29-Jun-2010	12	2.1	28-Jul-2010	8	1.4	29-Aug-2010	3	0.5
30-Jun-2010	9	1.6	29-Jul-2010	7	1.2			
			30-Jul-2010	3	0.5			
			31-Jul-2010	2	0.4			

[1]The day is the start date of a period in which data were recorded. Switching units in a day required a new period of data recording to begin. Thus, the table includes the same day listed twice for some respondents. The end dates associated with the start dates listed in the table vary, some time periods for which data were recorded ended the same day as the start date, others ended the following day.

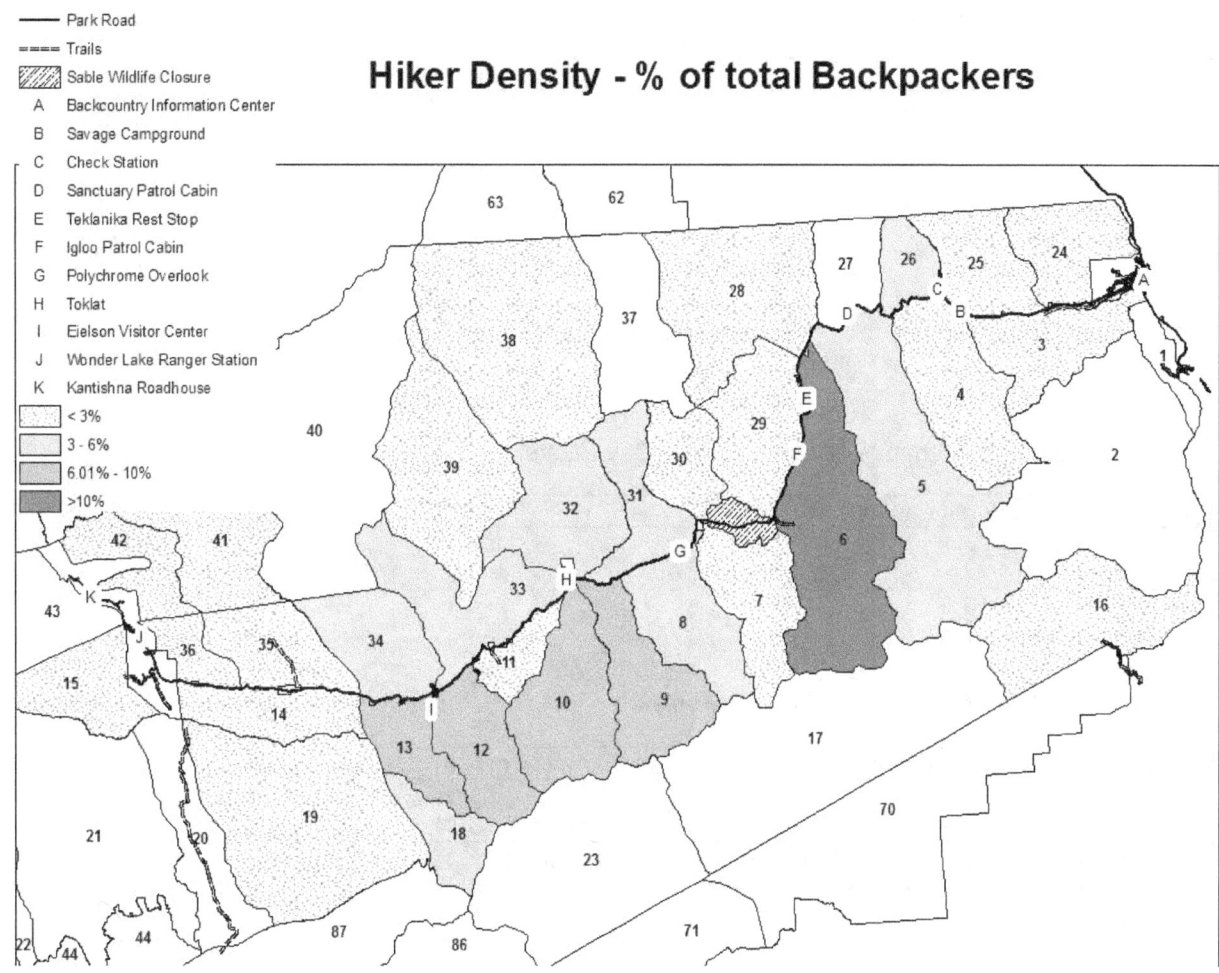

Figure 1. Distribution of Backpackers by Unit.

Day Hikers

Group Size of Day Hikers: Day hikers had a relatively wide distribution of group size (Table 16).

Table 16. Group Size of Day Hikers.

Group size	% of Day hikers[1]
1	12.2%
2	41.2%
3	10.8%
4	12.6%
5	4.1%
6-10	14%
>10	5.2%

[1] n was 565, includes respondents and non-respondents.

Length of Hike: The majority of day hikers hiked for 4 hours or less and hiked farther than ½ mile from the road, splitting their time on trails and off trails (Table 17 – Table 20).

Table 17. Length of Hike, Day Hikers.

Length of Hike[1]	Percentage[2]
1 hour or less	16.1%
1.01-2 hours	29.9%
2.01-3	18.6%
3.01-4	14.0%
4.01-5	11.3%
5.01-6	5.7%
Greater than 6	4.5%

[1]Hikes ranged in length from ¼ hour to 12 hours with a mean of 2.97 hours.
[2]n = 442

Table 18. Hiked Farther than ½ Mile From Road, Day Hikers.

Hiked more than ½ mile away from Road	Percent[1]
Yes	93.2%
No	6.8%

[1]n = 442

Table 19. Hiked on an Established Trail, Day Hikers.

Hiked on an Established Trail[1]	Percent[2]
Yes	52.0%
No	48.0%

[1]27 respondents (6.1%) checked both "Yes" and "No" but were included in the "Yes" category
[2]n = 444

Table 20. Time Spent Hiking Along Established Trail, Day Hikers.

Time Spent Hiking Along Established Trail[1]	Percent[2]
1 hour or less	39.6%
1.01-2 hours	38.3%
2.01-3	14.5%
Greater than 3 hours	7.5%

[1]Values for time spent hiking along an established trail ranged from .05 hours to 6.5 hours with a mean of 1.678 hours.
[2]n = 227

Units and Days of Day Hikers' Hikes: Day Hikers in the sampled hiked in 28 different units, with units 24 and 25 consisting of a high degree of on-trail hiking (Table 21). The days in which data were recorded for day hikers was constrained by sample times (i.e., backpackers reported hiking on days in which we did not sample, day hikers could only report on days we sampled). While at least one person hiked on every day sampled, the number of day hikers varied by day (Table 22).

Table 21. Units of Day Hikers and Characteristics of Hikes in those Units.

Units Visited			Within each Unit:					
Unit #[1]	# of Respondents[2]	% of Respondents	Hiked on Trail		Hiked off Trail		Hiked on and off Trail	
1	6	1.4%	6	100.0%				
2	1	0.2%	1	100.0%				
3	1	0.2%	1	100.0%				
4	6	1.4%	5	83.3%	1	16.7%		
5	2	0.5%			2	100.0%		
6	22	5.0%			22	100.0%		
7	3	0.7%	1	33.3%	2	66.7%		
8	11	2.5%	2	18.2%	9	81.8%		
9	10	2.3%			10	100.0%		
10	6	1.4%			6	100.0%		
11	33	7.4%			31	93.9%	2	6.1%
12	56	12.6%	32	57.1%	20	35.7%	4	7.1%
13	5	1.1%	1	20.0%	3	60.0%	1	20.0%
14	7	1.6%	4	42.9%	3	42.9%	1	14.3%
15	3	0.7%	3	100.0%				
20	1	0.2%	1	100.0%				
24	33	7.4%	31	93.9%	1	3.0%	1	3.0%
25	45	10.2%	41	91.1%	2	4.4%	2	4.4%
26	8	1.8%	2	25.0%	5	62.5%	1	12.5%
27	1	0.2%			1	100.0%		
28	5	1.1%	1	20.0%	3	60.0%	1	20.0%
29	27	6.1%	1	3.7%	26	96.3%		
30	7	1.6%	1	14.3%	6	85.7%		
31	25	5.6%	3	12.0%	21	84.0%	1	4.0%
32	12	2.7%			12	100.0%		
33	85	19.2%	56	65.9%	19	22.4%	10	11.8%
34	14	3.2%	9	69.2%	2	15.4%	2	15.4%
36	1	0.2%			1	100.0%		

[1] 7 Respondents (1.5%) hiked in multiple units.
[2] n=442

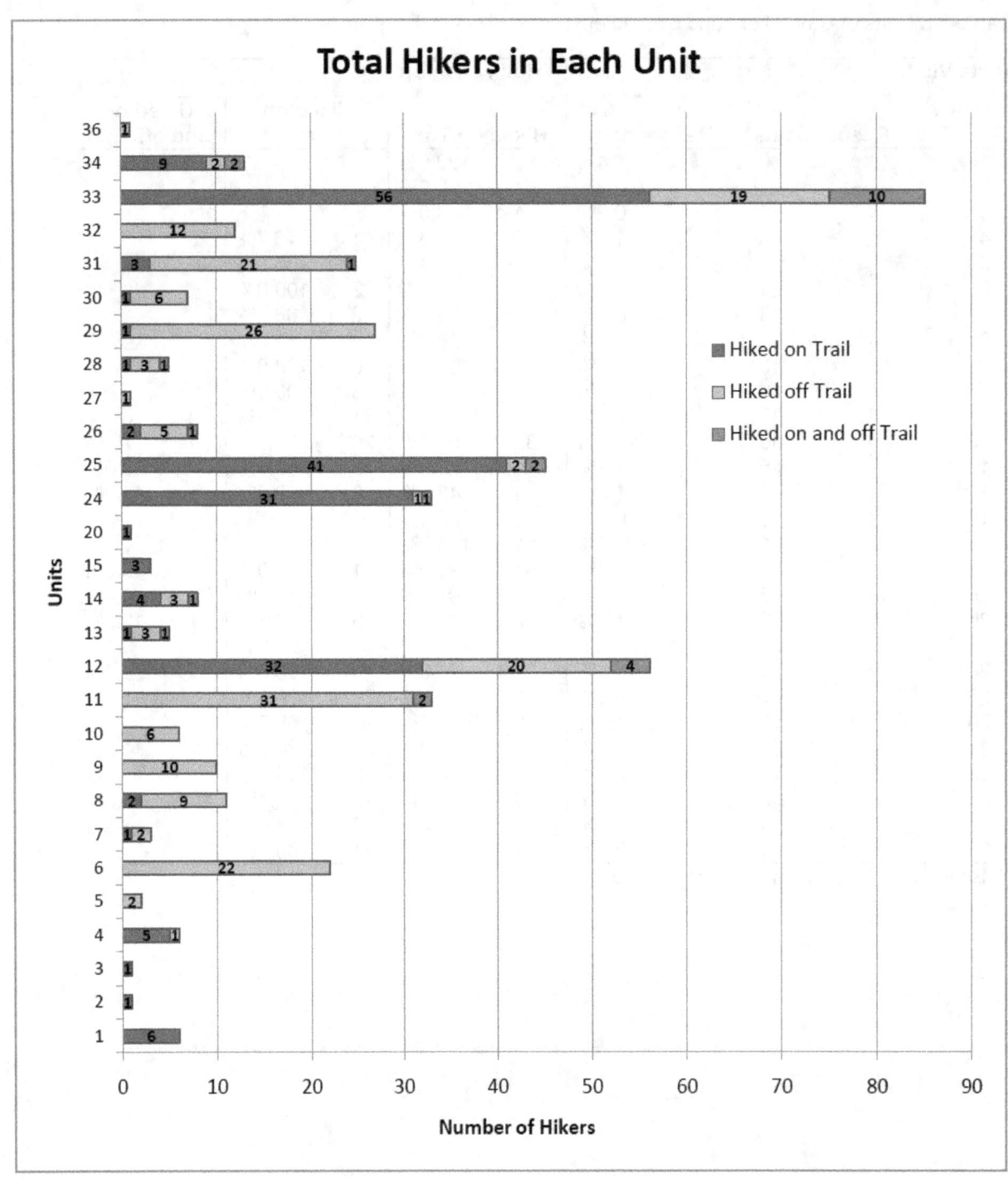

Figure 2. Number of Day Hikers by Unit.

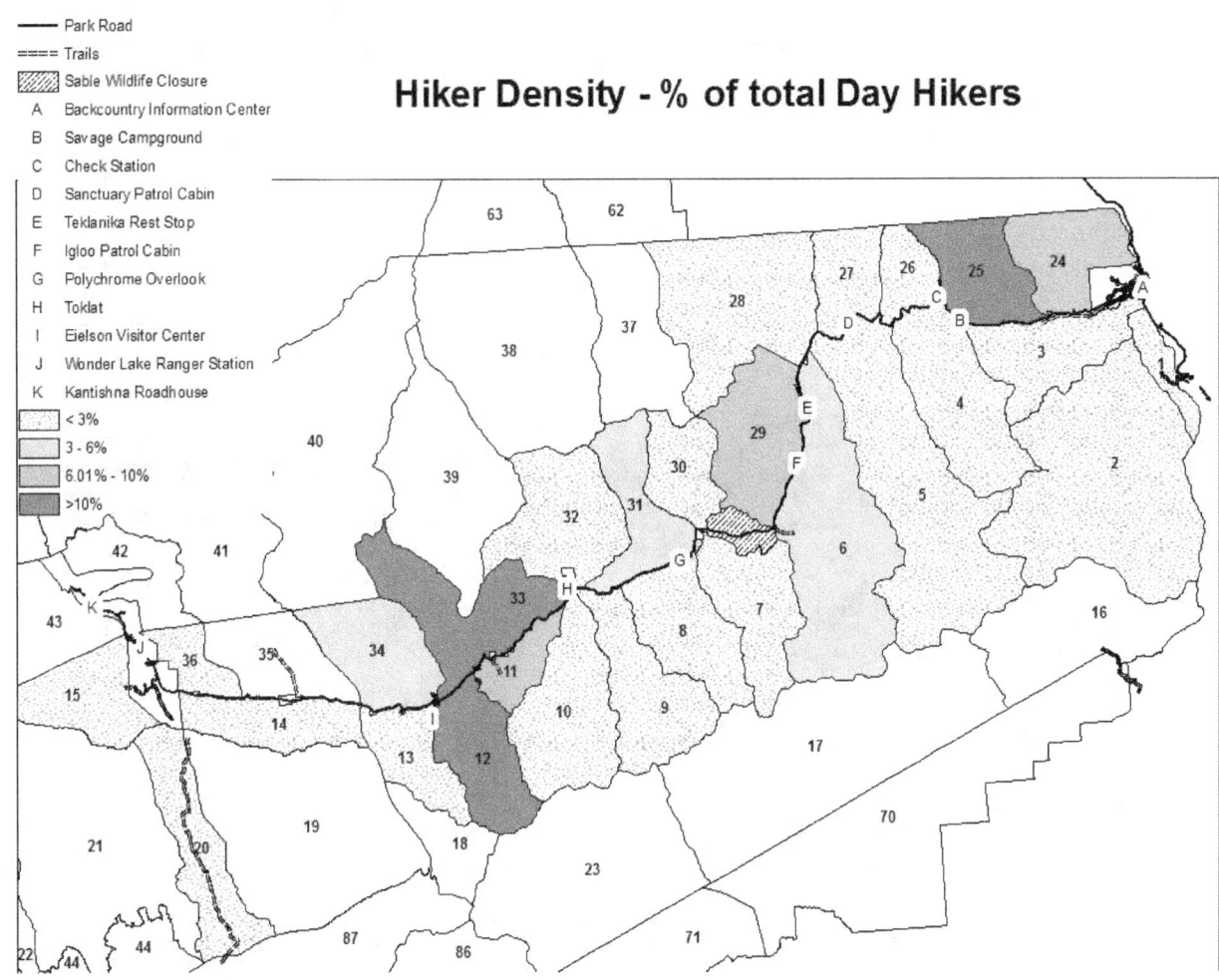

Figure 3. Percent of Day Hikers by Unit.

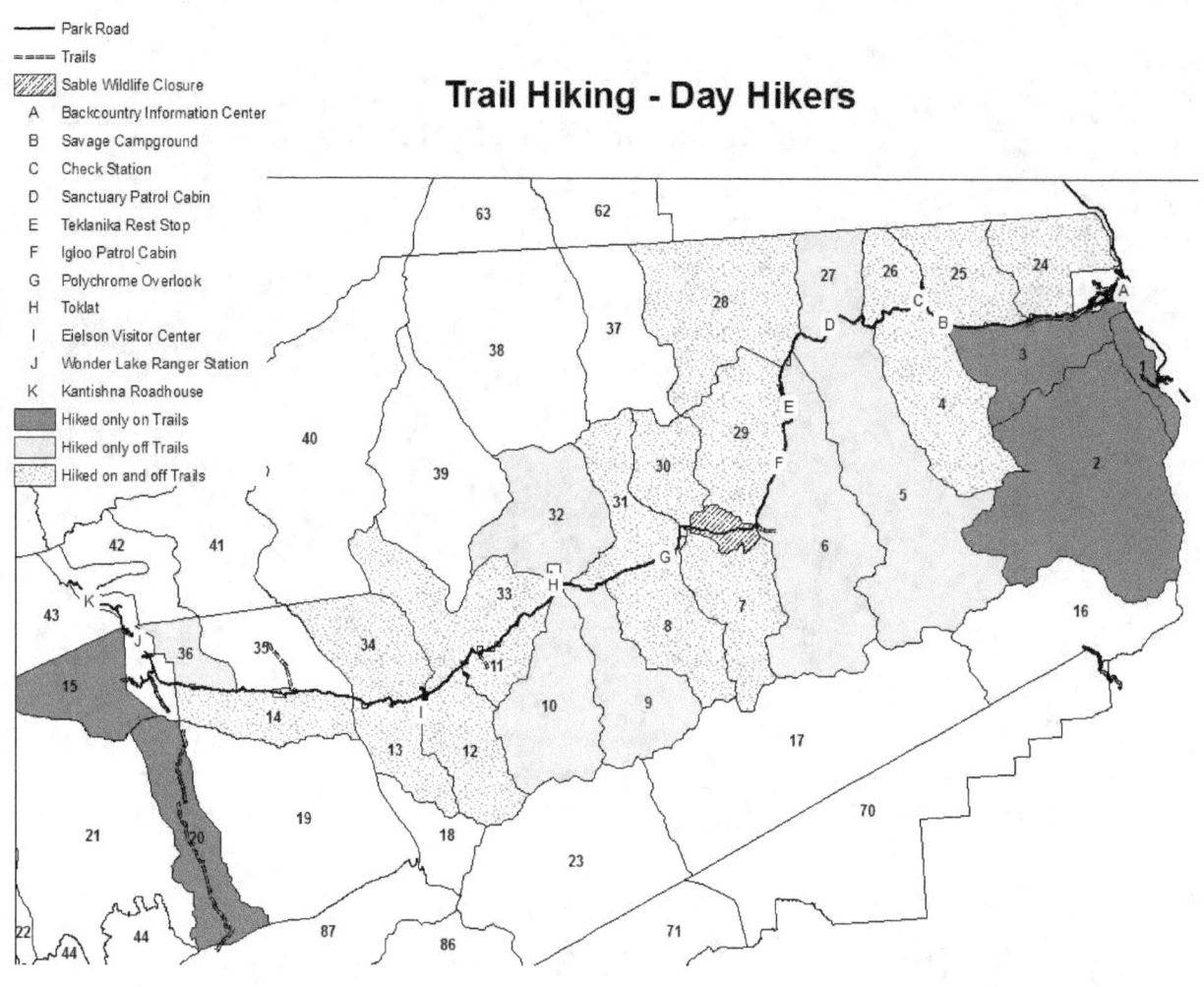

Figure 4. Distribution by Unit of Day Hikers That Hiked On or Off Trails.

Table 22. Days in which Data Were Recorded by Day Hikers.

Date	n	%	Date	n	%	Date	n	%
01-Jun-2010	3	0.7	01-Jul-2010	10	2.2	01-Aug-2010	9	2.0
02-Jun-2010	5	1.1	02-Jul-2010	7	1.6	02-Aug-2010	5	1.1
03-Jun-2010	4	0.9	03-Jul-2010	1	0.2	03-Aug-2010	1	0.2
05-Jun-2010	1	0.2	04-Jul-2010	7	1.6	07-Aug-2010	1	0.2
06-Jun-2010	2	0.4	05-Jul-2010	6	1.3	08-Aug-2010	5	1.1
07-Jun-2010	5	1.1	06-Jul-2010	11	2.5	09-Aug-2010	4	0.9
08-Jun-2010	5	1.1	07-Jul-2010	9	2.0	10-Aug-2010	7	1.6
09-Jun-2010	4	0.9	10-Jul-2010	6	1.3	11-Aug-2010	5	1.1
10-Jun-2010	1	0.2	11-Jul-2010	6	1.3	12-Aug-2010	12	2.7
12-Jun-2010	2	0.4	13-Jul-2010	9	2.0	13-Aug-2010	2	0.4
13-Jun-2010	4	0.9	14-Jul-2010	6	1.3	14-Aug-2010	10	2.2
15-Jun-2010	4	0.9	16-Jul-2010	1	0.2	15-Aug-2010	9	2.0
16-Jun-2010	5	1.1	18-Jul-2010	13	2.9	16-Aug-2010	9	2.0
17-Jun-2010	3	0.7	20-Jul-2010	12	2.7	17-Aug-2010	6	1.3
18-Jun-2010	6	1.3	22-Jul-2010	19	4.3	18-Aug-2010	7	1.6
19-Jun-2010	7	1.6	25-Jul-2010	12	2.7	19-Aug-2010	1	0.2
21-Jun-2010	6	1.3	26-Jul-2010	10	2.2	20-Aug-2010	5	1.1
22-Jun-2010	1	0.2	27-Jul-2010	7	1.6	21-Aug-2010	6	1.3
23-Jun-2010	9	2.0	28-Jul-2010	21	4.7	22-Aug-2010	3	0.7
24-Jun-2010	4	0.9	29-Jul-2010	11	2.5	23-Aug-2010	12	2.7
25-Jun-2010	1	0.2	31-Jul-2010	16	3.6	24-Aug-2010	2	0.4
27-Jun-2010	14	3.1				25-Aug-2010	9	2.0
28-Jun-2010	9	2.0				26-Aug-2010	3	0.7
29-Jun-2010	3	0.7				27-Aug-2010	2	0.4
30-Jun-2010	3	0.7						

Level of the Indicators and Comparison to the Standards

This section presents summary statistics of the indicators and compares the indicators to the standards. Three methods were used: 1) estimates of the mean levels of the indicators were compared to the standard, 2) how often individuals reported a level of the standard above the mean was calculated, and 3) the number of days in which a standard is violated was reported. Results are first presented for backpackers then for day hikers.

Table 23. Level of the Standard for Each Indicator in "OP1" Management Area.

Indicator	Standard
Encounters with motorized sound[1]	No more than one per day, audible less than 5% of any hour
Encounters with modern equipment	No more than one per day
Encounters with landscape modifications[2]	No landscape modifications are visible
Encounters with other park visitors	No more than two per day
Encounters with groups > 6	One or two per day[3]
Encounters with NPS researchers or rangers[4]	"Medium" routine patrols
Encounters with litter and human waste	Less than 5% reporting
Ability to camp out of sight or sound of others	Always

[1]For units 41 & 42 the standard for motorized sound is no more than 10 encounters per day and motorized sound might be audible up to 15% of any hour.
[2]As defined in "Table 1: Management Area Descriptions" in the BCMP summary (National Park Service n.d.), which lists the standard as "low 1 encounter/day." This differs from "Table 2. Key to the Management Area Descriptors" in the BCMP summary which lists the standard for low as no more than 1 encounter per trip. No more than one per day will be used throughout this report.
[3]As stated in the BCMP. However, in this report two will be used as the standard.
[4]For units 41 & 42 the standard for encounters with NPS rangers or researchers is "low" occasional patrols.

Notes Regarding Data Analysis

For both backpackers and day hikers analysis is presented by unit. However, many units have a very low number of responses. This lowers the confidence in generalizing to all hikers in those units. When presenting means or percentages the 95% confidence interval is presented, illustrating the wide margin of error for some units. If a unit had a small n and the results showed none of the standards for the unit were violated, one would have little confidence that the results could be generalized to all users of the unit.

Outliers were not removed from the analysis. The tables presenting the mean level of the indicators also present the range and median which can be used to assess the influence of outliers. While some responses were outliers using a definition of greater than four standard deviations from the mean, they were determined to be within the range of possibility and thus were retained in all analysis.

A critical note regarding a difference in the measured level of the indicators and the standards should guide comparison of the indicators to the standards. The initial conceptualization of the survey and the development of the questions that followed explicitly included impacts originating in the road corridor. However, the standards include only impacts originating within the backcountry, i.e., they exclude impacts originating in the road corridor. Therefore, the level of the indicators might be overstated.

There were two versions of the descriptor of landscape modifications in the question asking respondents to report the number of landscape modifications they encountered. The second version of the descriptor added the qualifier that landscape modifications included constructed and human caused (as opposed to an earlier version that just said "trails") and instructed respondents to exclude animal trails. There was no significant difference in the number of landscape modifications reported on the different versions of the surveys. For backpackers the mean number of landscape modifications reported on the first survey and the second version with additional clarification on what to include/exclude as a landscape modification was 1.0 and 1.3, respectively (t [302, 129] = -1.2, p = 0.218). For day hikers the mean number of landscape modifications reported on the first survey and the second version with additional clarification on what to include/exclude as a landscape modification was 1.7 and 2.2, respectively (t [198, 184] = -1.32, p = 0.187). Five backpackers, who were given the first version, were asked how they interpreted "landscape modification." A key in their definition was a path and surface. The responses were as follows.

- Followable path, any surface is fine
- Prefer natural path to follow
- A path to walk on, any surface
- Human made path within an otherwise natural area
- Any linear feature trampled down, any "surface"

While some of the five definitions allow for the possibility of including animal trail, the mean number of landscape modifications reported on the two versions indicated the question wording did not have an effect. The two versions of the landscape modification questions were combined in the analysis.

Backpackers

Overall Mean Levels of Indicators: Overall, the mean level of motorized sounds and landscape modifications exceed the standards, the percent of visitors reporting litter and human waste is above the standard, and there were 31 nights in which backpackers did not camp out of sight or sound of others. The 95% confidence interval for equipment encounters includes the standard, and the levels of other park visitors, number of groups larger than six, and encounters with NPS rangers or researchers are below the standard.

Table 24. Overall Mean Level of Indicators, Backpackers.

	n	Mean	Median	Max	Standard Deviation	Lower 95% CI	Upper 95% CI
Motorized sound[1]	525	3.21	2	40	4.16	2.85	3.56
Equipment encounters	529	1.00	0	27	2.70	0.77	1.23
Landscape modifications	537	1.04	1	25	1.73	0.89	1.18
Other park visitors	535	0.77	0	15	1.58	0.63	0.90
Number of groups > 6	552	0.04	0	2	0.21	0.02	0.05
Encounters with NPS	550	0.03	0	1	0.17	0.02	0.04
The indicators below are expressed as a percentage rather than a mean							
See litter/human waste	564	11.2%			n/a	8.4%	13.6%
Able to camp out of sight/sound of others	438[2]	93%[3]			n/a	90.6	94.9

[1]Includes August 24 & 25, in which a search and rescue operation took place; responses on those dates were: Aug. 24, 7 motorized sounds 1 time; Aug 25, 1 motorized sound 1 time and 2 motorized sounds 2 times.
[2]The n was adjusted for respondents who recorded a night camping on two pages, i.e., they responded to the question in the evening and the morning of the next day.
[3]There were 31 nights in which people reported they did not camp out of sight or sound of others.

Mean Levels of / Percent Reporting Indicators by Unit: Results for the indicators are presented by unit. As noted in the discussion for each table, units with low sample sizes have low statistical power to detect differences.

Motorized Sound: standard = no more than one per day.
- Examining units with n > = 10 (n = 18), reveals 13 units with 95% confidence intervals (CI) of the means above one.
- However, for the five units with n > = 10 and 95% CIs that overlap one, statistical power is low, and, thus, there is a high probability of incorrectly concluding the standard is not violated.

Table 25. Mean Level of Motorized Sound Reported by Backpackers, by Unit.

Unit	n	Mean	Median	Max	SD	95% CI lower	95% CI upper
3	1	10.00	10	10	-	-	-
4	13	3.15	2	10	3.65	1.17	5.14
5	18	6.00	6	14	3.80	4.24	7.76
6	60	3.68	3	20	3.06	2.91	4.46
7	15	7.93	5	40	10.49	2.62	13.24
8	15	4.67	3	20	5.19	2.04	7.29
9	46	3.70	3	20	3.99	2.54	4.85
10	51	3.73	2	23	4.25	2.56	4.89
11	15	2.20	2	7	2.11	1.13	3.27
12	34	3.88	2	30	5.63	1.99	5.77
13	34	3.85	3	15	3.73	2.60	5.11
14	1	0.00	0	0	-	-	-
15	7	0.86	0	4	1.46	-0.23	1.94
16	1	1.00	1	1	-	-	-
18	23	2.96	1	15	3.95	1.34	4.57
19	5	1.80	2	5	2.05	0.00	3.60
24	2	2.50	2.5	5	3.54	-2.40	7.40
25	2	0.00	0	0	0.00	0.00	0.00
26	18	3.11	.5	25	6.09	0.30	5.92
28	5	2.20	1	6	2.68	-0.15	4.55
29	11	5.73	4	10	3.38	3.73	7.72
30	3	1.00	1	2	1.00	-0.13	2.13
31	25	1.80	1	9	2.31	0.89	2.71
32	31	2.03	1	15	2.81	1.04	3.02
33	27	1.56	1	7	2.19	0.73	2.38
34	20	1.25	.5	5	1.59	0.56	1.94
35	9	1.00	0	7	2.35	-0.53	2.53
36	1	3.00	3	3	-	-	-
38	3	1.67	2	3	1.53	-0.06	3.40
39	16	1.25	1	4	1.13	0.70	1.80
41[1]	2	0.00	0	0	0.00	0.00	0.00
42[1]	9	1.89	2	5	2.03	0.56	3.21

[1]The standard for units 41 and 42 is no more than 10 encounters per day.

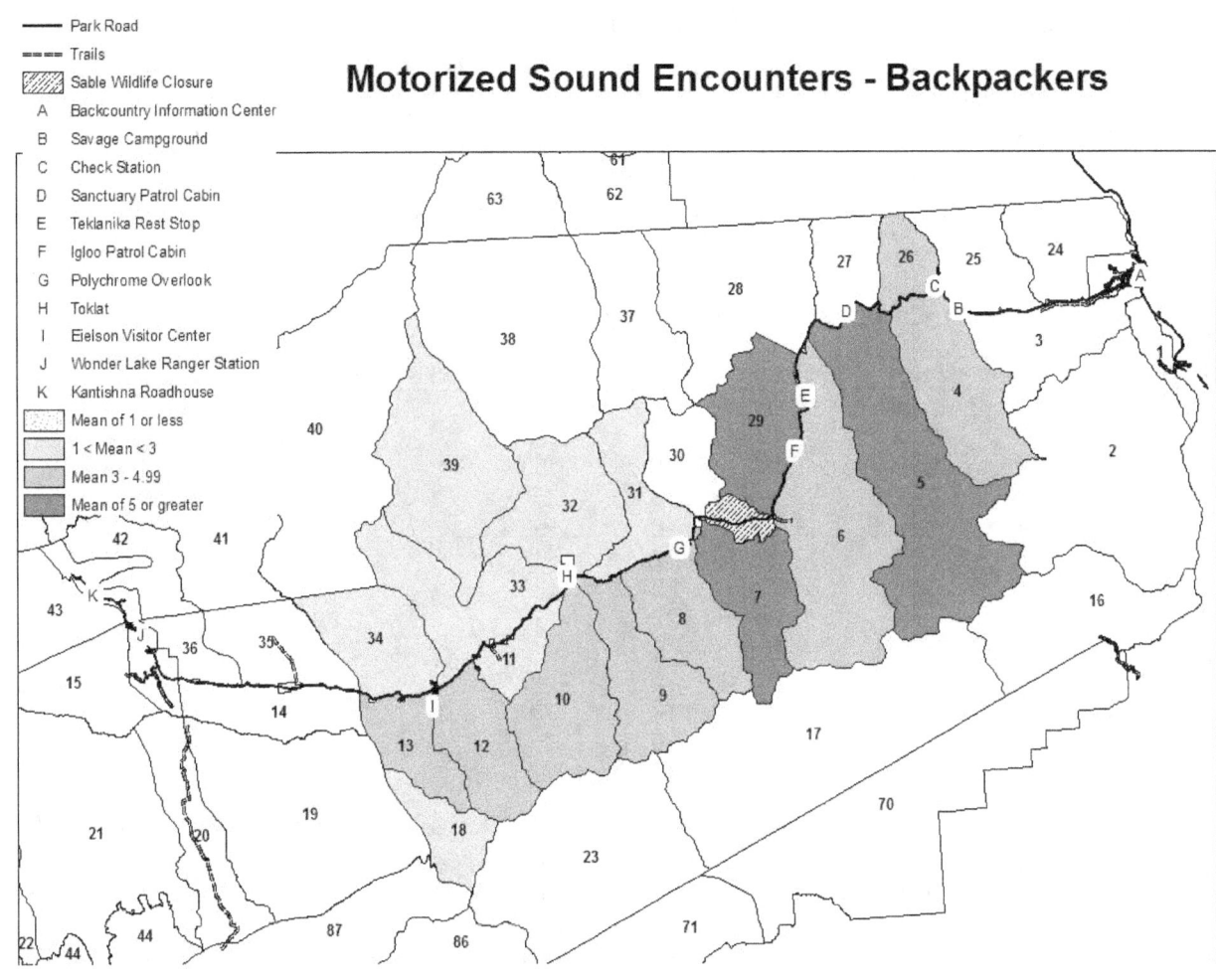

Figure 5. Distribution of Mean Level of Motorized Sound as Reported by Backpackers, for Units with n > = 10

Modern Equipment: standard = no more than one per day.

- Examining units with n > = 10 (n = 18), reveals one unit with a 95% confidence intervals (CI) of the mean above one.
- However, for the nine units with n > = 10 and 95% CIs that overlap one, statistical power is low (because of high standard deviations in some cases and low *n*s in other cases), and, thus, there is a high probability of incorrectly concluding the standard is not violated.

Table 26. Mean Level of Encounters with Modern Equipment Reported by Backpackers, by Unit.

Unit	n	Mean	Median	Max	SD	95% CI lower	95% CI upper
3	1	3.00	3	3	-	-	-
4	15	0.33	0	2	0.62	0.02	0.65
5	18	0.67	0	5	1.50	-0.02	1.36
6	60	0.43	0	10	1.54	0.04	0.82
7	14	1.57	0	8	2.59	0.21	2.93
8	16	3.56	1	12	4.82	1.20	5.92
9	45	1.56	0	20	3.68	0.48	2.63
10	50	1.94	0	27	4.51	0.69	3.19
11	15	0.00	0	0	0.00	0.00	0.00
12	34	0.65	0	5	1.30	0.21	1.08
13	35	1.17	0	10	2.19	0.45	1.90
14	1	0.00	0	0	-	-	-
15	7	1.43	0	10	3.78	-1.37	4.23
16	1	0.00	0	0	-	-	-
18	24	0.29	0	6	1.23	-0.20	0.78
19	6	0.50	0	2	0.84	-0.17	1.17
24	2	0.50	0.5	1	0.71	-0.48	1.48
25	2	0.00	0	0	0.00	0.00	0.00
26	18	2.06	0	20	5.08	-0.29	4.40
28	5	2.40	0	8	3.58	-0.74	5.54
29	11	2.36	0	10	3.23	0.45	4.27
30	3	0.00	0	0	0.00	0.00	0.00
31	25	0.16	0	1	0.37	0.01	0.31
32	29	1.38	0	15	3.24	0.20	2.56
33	28	0.07	0	1	0.26	-0.03	0.17
34	21	0.48	0	2	0.68	0.19	0.77
35	9	0.44	0	2	0.73	-0.03	0.92
36	1	3.00	3	3	-	-	-
38	3	0.00	0	0	0.00	0.00	0.00
39	15	0.00	0	0	0.00	0.00	0.00
41	3	0.00	0	0	0.00	0.00	0.00
42	9	1.22	1	3	1.20	0.44	2.01

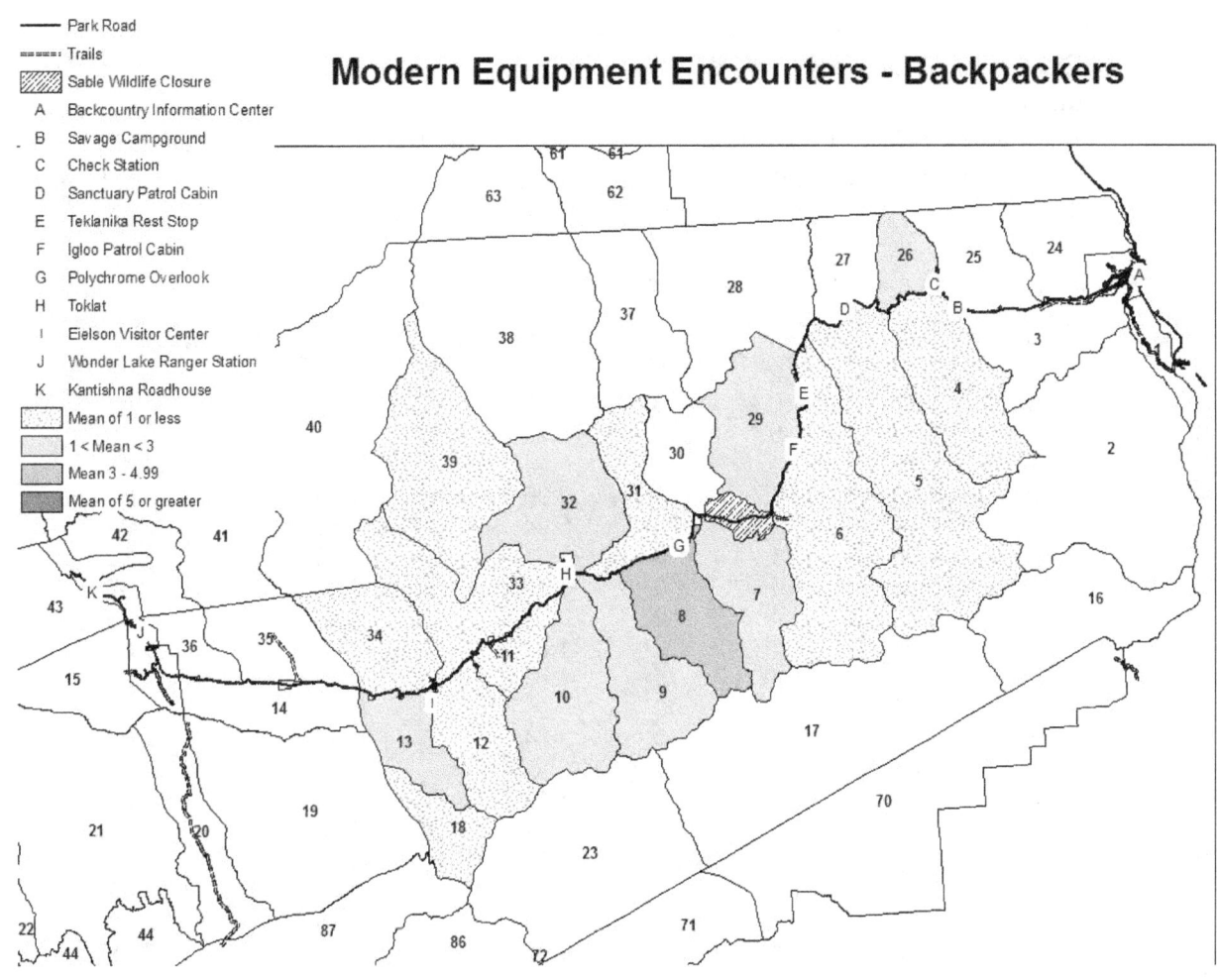

Figure 6. Distribution of Mean Level of Modern Equipment as Reported by Backpackers, for Units with n > = 10.

Landscape Modifications: standard = none visible.
- Examining units with n > = 10, reveals 15 units with 95% confidence intervals (CI) of the mean above zero.
- However, for the 3 units with n > = 10 and 95% CIs that overlap zero, statistical power is low (of these three units, unit 33 has the highest power at 0.60), and, thus, there is a high probability of incorrectly concluding the standard is not violated.

Table 27. Mean Level of Landscape Modifications Reported by Backpackers, by Unit.

Unit	n	Mean	Median	Max	SD	95% CI lower	95% CI upper
3	2	2.00	2	3	1.41	0.04	3.96
4	15	0.67	0	3	0.90	0.21	1.12
5	19	0.63	0	3	1.12	0.13	1.13
6	62	1.13	1	6	1.44	0.77	1.49
7	15	1.07	1	3	0.96	0.58	1.55
8	17	2.47	1	25	5.94	-0.35	5.29
9	46	0.98	1	6	1.31	0.60	1.36
10	49	1.18	1	5	1.38	0.80	1.57
11	15	0.73	1	2	0.59	0.43	1.03
12	34	1.09	1	5	1.22	0.68	1.50
13	35	1.20	1	5	1.23	0.79	1.61
14	1	0.00	0	0	-	-	-
15	7	1.57	0	10	3.74	-1.20	4.34
16	1	0.00	0	0	-	-	-
18	24	0.79	0	3	1.18	0.32	1.26
19	6	0.17	0	1	0.41	-0.16	0.49
24	2	0.50	.5	1	0.71	-0.48	1.48
25	2	0.50	.5	1	0.71	-0.48	1.48
26	18	1.56	1	5	1.25	0.98	2.13
28	5	1.00	1	2	1.00	0.12	1.88
29	11	2.00	2	4	1.26	1.25	2.75
30	3	2.33	2	3	0.58	1.68	2.99
31	25	0.88	1	3	0.73	0.60	1.16
32	31	1.19	0	12	2.34	0.37	2.02
33	28	0.21	0	2	0.57	0.00	0.42
34	21	0.76	0	3	0.94	0.36	1.17
35	9	0.33	0	1	0.50	0.01	0.66
36	1	0.00	0	0	-	-	-
38	3	0.00	0	0	0.00	0.00	0.00
39	15	0.13	0	2	0.52	-0.13	0.39
41	3	1.33	1	2	0.58	0.68	1.99
42	9	1.44	1	3	0.73	0.97	1.92

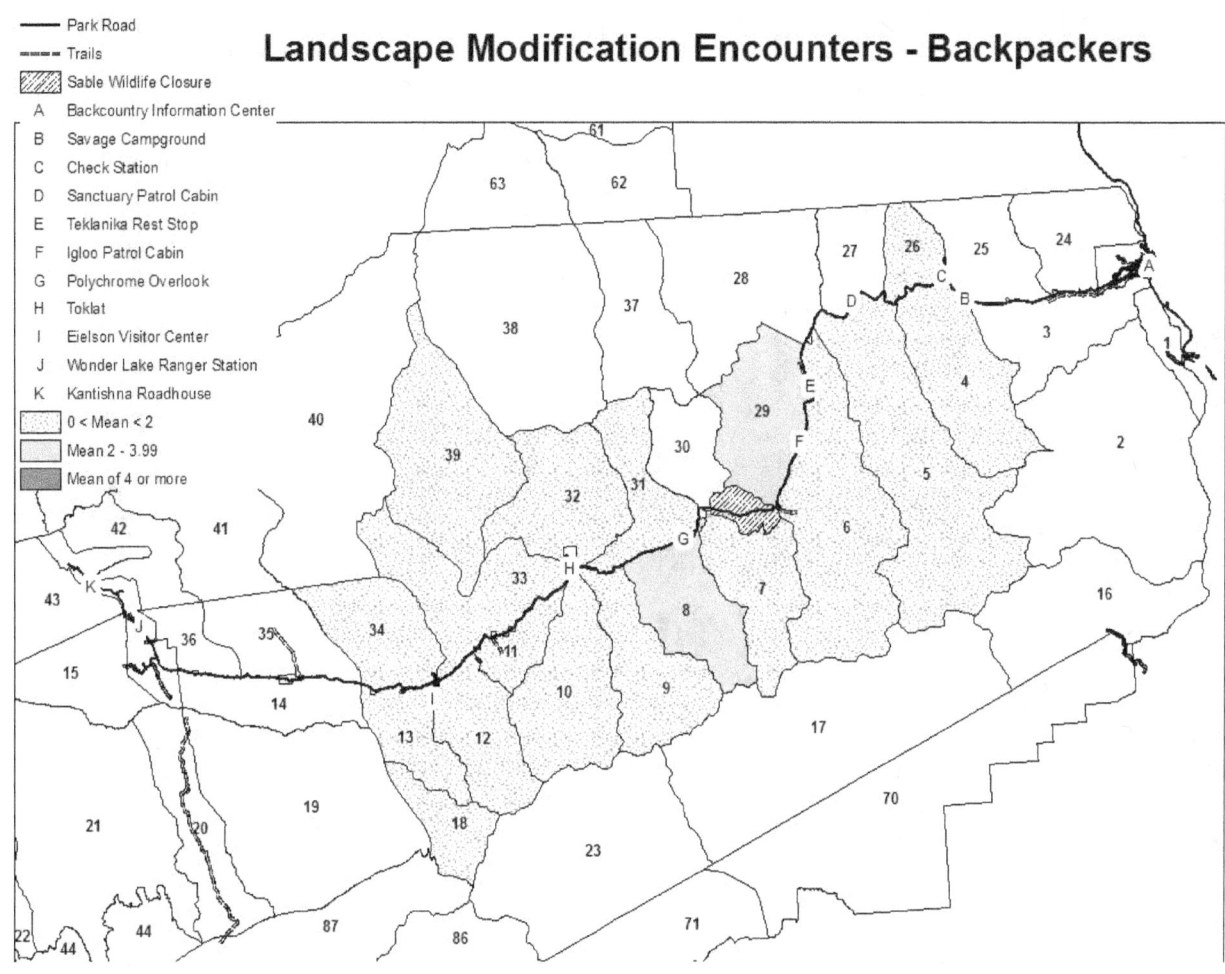

Figure 7. Distribution of Mean Level of Landscape Modifications as Reported by Backpackers, for Units with n > = 10.

Other Park Visitors: standard = no more than two.

- Examining units with n > = 10 (n = 18), reveals one unit with a 95% CI of the mean that overlaps two, all other 95% CIs were less than two.

Table 28. Mean Level of Encounters with Other Park Visitors Reported by Backpackers, by Unit.

Unit	n	Mean	Median	Max	SD	95% CI lower	95% CI upper
3	2	0.00	0	0	0.00	0.00	0.00
4	15	0.33	0	2	0.62	0.02	0.65
5	18	0.33	0	4	0.97	-0.11	0.78
6	61	1.03	0	15	2.44	0.42	1.65
7	15	0.13	0	1	0.35	-0.04	0.31
8	18	1.11	1	5	1.32	0.50	1.72
9	45	0.62	0	3	0.78	0.40	0.85
10	51	1.22	1	5	1.29	0.86	1.57
11	14	0.57	0	2	0.85	0.13	1.02
12	35	0.94	0	10	1.91	0.31	1.58
13	34	0.91	0	4	1.22	0.50	1.32
14	1	1.00	1	1	-	-	-
15	7	1.14	1	4	1.46	0.06	2.23
16	1	0.00	0	0	-	-	-
18	24	0.33	0	2	0.56	0.11	0.56
19	6	1.67	0	10	4.08	-1.60	4.93
24	2	5.00	5	10	7.07	-4.80	14.80
25	2	0.00	0	0	0.00	0.00	0.00
26	18	1.56	1	10	2.48	0.41	2.70
28	5	0.00	0	0	0.00	0.00	0.00
29	11	0.73	0	2	0.90	0.19	1.26
30	3	0.33	0	1	0.58	-0.32	0.99
31	25	0.44	0	1	0.51	0.24	0.64
32	31	0.23	0	1	0.43	0.08	0.38
33	29	0.62	0	2	0.73	0.36	0.89
34	21	0.48	0	2	0.68	0.19	0.77
35	9	0.11	0	1	0.33	-0.11	0.33
36	1	0.00	0	0	-	-	-
38	3	0.00	0	0	0.00	0.00	0.00
39	15	0.33	0	1	0.49	0.09	0.58
41	2	0.50	.5	1	0.71	-0.48	1.48
42	9	2.56	1	15	4.77	-0.56	5.67

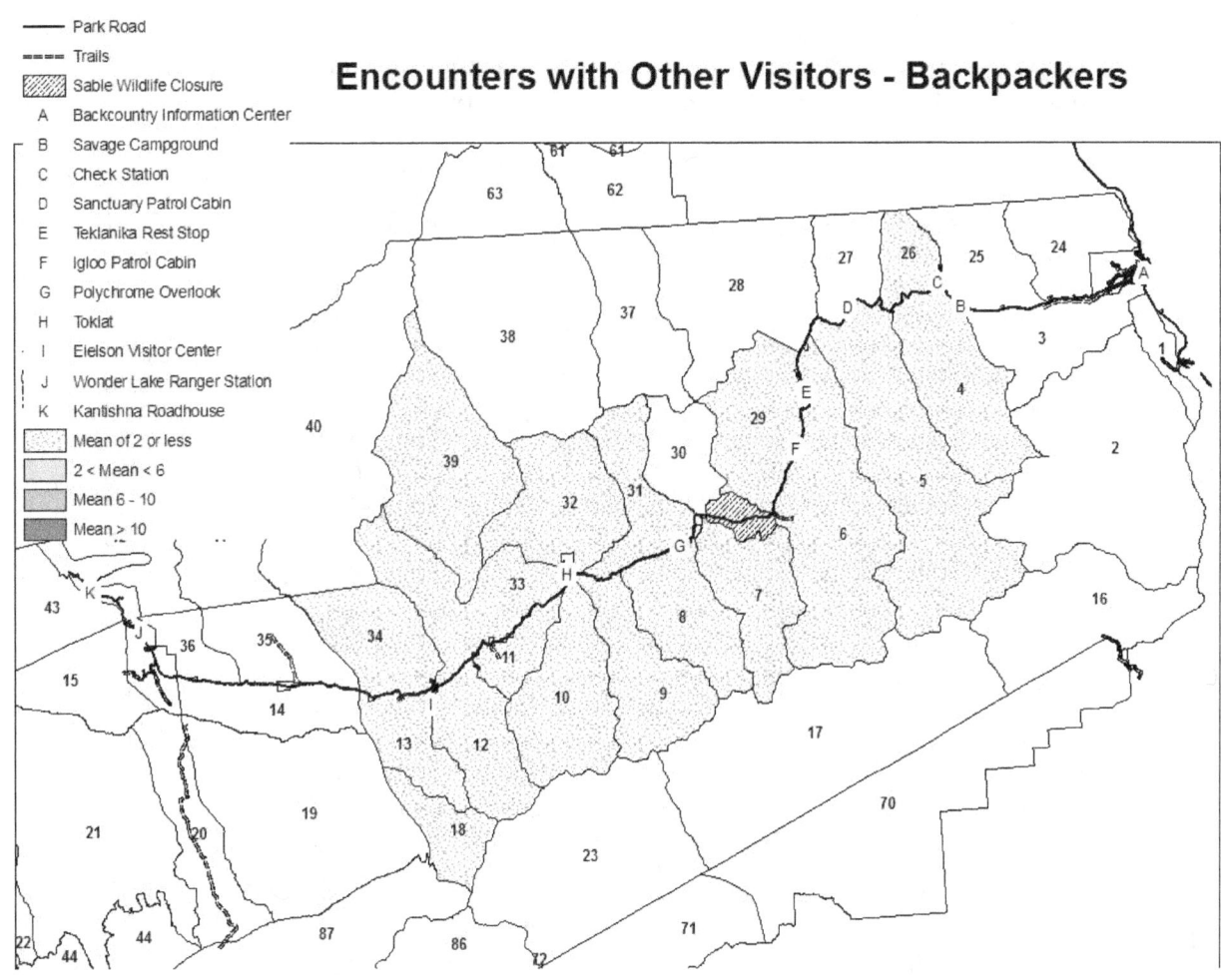

Figure 8. Distribution of Mean Level of Encounters with Other Visitors Reported by Backpackers, for Units with n > = 10.

Large Groups: standard = no more than two.
- Examining units with n > = 10 (n = 18), reveals no units with 95% confidence intervals (CI) of the mean above, or overlapping, two.

Table 29. Mean Level of Encounters with Groups > 6 Reported by Backpackers, by Unit.

Unit	n	Mean	Median	Max	SD	95% CI lower	95% CI upper
3	2	0.00	0	0	0.00	0.00	0.00
4	15	0.00	0	0	0.00	0.00	0.00
5	19	0.00	0	0	0.00	0.00	0.00
6	61	0.07	0	2	0.31	-0.01	0.14
7	16	0.00	0	0	0.00	0.00	0.00
8	20	0.00	0	0	0.00	0.00	0.00
9	48	0.04	0	1	0.20	-0.02	0.10
10	51	0.02	0	1	0.14	-0.02	0.06
11	15	0.20	0	2	0.56	-0.08	0.48
12	38	0.03	0	1	0.16	-0.03	0.08
13	34	0.00	0	0	0.00	0.00	0.00
14	1	0.00	0	0	-	-	-
15	6	0.00	0	0	0.00	0.00	0.00
16	1	0.00	0	0	-	-	-
18	24	0.00	0	0	0.00	0.00	0.00
19	5	0.00	0	0	0.00	0.00	0.00
24	3	0.00	0	0	0.00	0.00	0.00
25	2	0.00	0	0	0.00	0.00	0.00
26	18	0.11	0	1	0.32	-0.04	0.26
28	5	0.00	0	0	0.00	0.00	0.00
29	12	0.08	0	1	0.29	-0.08	0.25
30	3	0.33	0	1	0.58	-0.32	0.99
31	25	0.00	0	0	0.00	0.00	0.00
32	31	0.00	0	0	0.00	0.00	0.00
33	30	0.07	0	1	0.25	-0.02	0.16
34	22	0.05	0	1	0.21	-0.04	0.13
35	9	0.00	0	0	0.00	0.00	0.00
36	2	0.00	0	0	0.00	0.00	0.00
38	3	0.00	0	0	0.00	0.00	0.00
39	16	0.00	0	0	0.00	0.00	0.00
41	2	0.00	0	0	0.00	0.00	0.00
42	9	0.22	0	2	0.67	-0.21	0.66

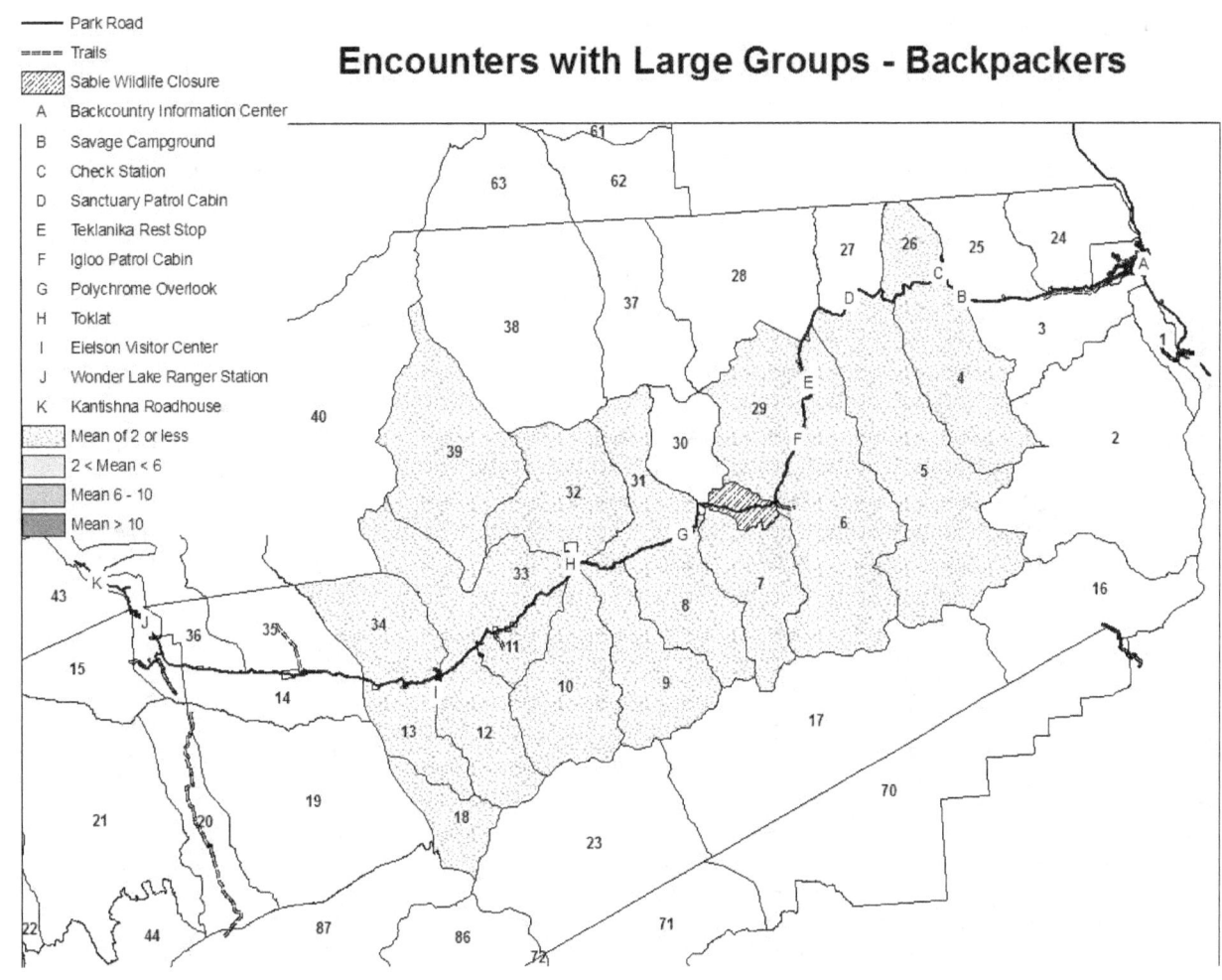

Encounters with Large Groups - Backpackers

Legend:
- Park Road
- Trails
- Sable Wildlife Closure
- A Backcountry Information Center
- B Savage Campground
- C Check Station
- D Sanctuary Patrol Cabin
- E Teklanika Rest Stop
- F Igloo Patrol Cabin
- G Polychrome Overlook
- H Toklat
- I Eielson Visitor Center
- J Wonder Lake Ranger Station
- K Kantishna Roadhouse
- Mean of 2 or less
- 2 < Mean < 6
- Mean 6 - 10
- Mean > 10

Figure 9. Distribution of Mean Level of Encounters with Groups > 6 as Reported by Backpackers, for Units with n > = 10.

NPS Rangers or Researchers: standard = routine patrols.

- The mean level of encounters is very low, and all units appear to be in compliance with the standard.

Table 30. Mean Level of Encounters with NPS Rangers or Researchers Reported by Backpackers, by Unit.

Unit	n	Mean	Median	Max	SD	95% CI lower	95% CI upper
3	2	0.50	0.5	1	0.71	-0.48	1.48
4	15	0.07	0.0	1	0.26	-0.06	0.20
5	19	0.00	0.0	0	0.00	0.00	0.00
6	62	0.02	0.0	1	0.13	-0.02	0.05
7	16	0.00	0.0	0	0.00	0.00	0.00
8	20	0.10	0.0	1	0.31	-0.03	0.23
9	48	0.00	0.0	0	0.00	0.00	0.00
10	51	0.06	0.0	1	0.24	-0.01	0.12
11	15	0.00	0.0	0	0.00	0.00	0.00
12	38	0.00	0.0	0	0.00	0.00	0.00
13	33	0.00	0.0	0	0.00	0.00	0.00
14	1	0.00	0.0	0	-	-	-
15	7	0.14	0.0	1	0.38	-0.14	0.42
18	24	0.08	0.0	1	0.28	-0.03	0.20
19	5	0.20	0.0	1	0.45	-0.19	0.59
24	2	0.00	0.0	0	0.00	0.00	0.00
25	2	0.00	0.0	0	0.00	0.00	0.00
26	18	0.00	0.0	0	0.00	0.00	0.00
28	5	0.00	0.0	0	0.00	0.00	0.00
29	12	0.00	0.0	0	0.00	0.00	0.00
30	3	0.33	0.0	1	0.58	-0.32	0.99
31	25	0.00	0.0	0	0.00	0.00	0.00
32	31	0.06	0.0	1	0.25	-0.02	0.15
33	29	0.00	0.0	0	0.00	0.00	0.00
34	22	0.00	0.0	0	0.00	0.00	0.00
35	9	0.00	0.0	0	0.00	0.00	0.00
36	2	0.00	0.0	0	0.00	0.00	0.00
38	3	0.00	0.0	0	0.00	0.00	0.00
39	16	0.00	0.0	0	0.00	0.00	0.00
41[1]	2	0.00	0.0	0	0.00	0.00	0.00
42[1]	9	0.00	0.0	0	0.00	0.00	0.00

[1]Standard is occasional ranger patrols.

Litter or Human Waste: standard = less than 5% reporting.

- Examining units with n > = 10 (n = 17), reveals two units with 95% confidence intervals (CI) of the proportion above 5%.
- However, for the units with n > = 10 and 95% CIs that overlap 5%, statistical power is low and, thus, there is a high probability of incorrectly concluding the standard is not violated

Table 31. Percent of Backpackers Reporting Seeing Litter or Human Waste, by Unit.

Unit	n	Saw litter or human waste	Estimated population[1]	95% CI lower	95% CI upper
3	2	50.0%	18	-17.2%	117.2%
4	15	13.3%	132	-2.9%	29.5%
5	19	0.0%	167	0.0%	0.0%
6	63	9.5%	553	2.7%	16.3%
7	16	12.5%	141	-2.8%	27.8%
8	20	15.0%	176	0.2%	29.8%
9	48	4.2%	422	-1.2%	9.6%
10	52	11.5%	457	3.3%	19.7%
11	15	0.0%	132	0.0%	0.0%
12	38	10.5%	334	1.3%	19.7%
13	35	17.1%	307	5.3%	28.9%
14	1	0.0%	9	0.0%	0.0%
15	7	0.0%	61	0.0%	0.0%
16	1	0.0%	9	0.0%	0.0%
18	24	16.7%	211	2.6%	30.8%
19	6	0.0%	53	0.0%	0.0%
24	3	33.3%	26	-17.9%	84.5%
25	2	0.0%	18	0.0%	0.0%
26	18	5.6%	158	-4.4%	15.6%
28	5	20.0%	44	-13.4%	53.4%
29	12	16.7%	105	-3.3%	36.7%
30	3	0.0%	26	0.0%	0.0%
31	26	11.5%	228	-0.1%	23.1%
32	33	18.2%	290	5.8%	30.6%
33	31	9.7%	272	-0.1%	19.5%
34	23	8.7%	202	-2.2%	19.6%
35	9	11.1%	79	-8.3%	30.5%
36	2	0.0%	18	0.0%	0.0%
38	3	66.7%	26	15.6%	117.9%
39	16	12.5%	141	-2.8%	27.8%
41	3	0.0%	26	0.0%	0.0%
42	9	22.2%	79	-3.5%	47.9%

[1]The data from the survey is a unique day of hiking (with some exceptions for multiple units in one day). The confidence interval needs to account for the total population, so an estimate of total population (i.e., "estimated population") was calculated as follows.

- 1405 permits were issued in June, July, and August of 2010.
- An average length of hike of 3.5 days per permit (as one survey was completed per permit) was assumed based on survey results, for a total number of days hiked by permit of 4918.
- The distribution of days hiked in the survey results was assumed to be representative of the population proportions.
- Each unit's percent in the sample was multiplied by 4918 to estimate the total population of days hiked by permit for each unit.

Camping Out of Sight or Sound of Others: Standard = always.

- There were 31 nights in which respondents reported they did not camp out of sight or sound of others.
- Note, the question did not ask if they were unable to camp at their first choice of campsite because someone was already there.

Table 32. Number of Backpackers Not Camping Out of Sight or Sound of Others, by Unit.

Unit	# not able to camp out of sight or sound[1]	Unit	# not able to camp out of sight or sound
3	1	24	0
4	0	25	0
5	0	26	0
6	3	28	0
7	1	29	3
8	5	30	0
9	4	31	3
10	1	32	0
11	0	33	3
12	2	34	1
13	0	35	1
14	0	36	0
15	0	38	0
16	0	39	1
18	0	41	0
19	0	42	1

[1]One of the 31 responses of not being able to camp out of sight or sound did not specify the unit.

Factors Influencing Mean Levels of Indicators for Backpackers:
Distance from Road: Backpackers were likely to see a higher level of landscape modifications near the park road. Note, the survey did not exclude the park road as viewed from a backcountry unit. Backpackers also encountered more NPS personnel near the park road, but the magnitude is not of practical significance. Motorized sound encounters showed a significant difference at alpha = 10%, with the number of sound encounters being higher away from the road (Table 33). This could be attributed to longer periods of time being spent away from the road.

Table 33. Influence of being Near or Away from Park Road on Indicators.

	Near road[1]	Away from road	t	p
Motorized sound encounters				
Mean	2.98	3.61	1.65	0.10
N	343	178		
Std. Dev.	4.17	4.16		
Modern equipment encounters				
Mean	1.08	0.79	-1.19	0.234
N	342	182		
Std. Dev.	2.59	2.85		
Landscape modifications				
Mean	1.25	.62	-4.07	<0.001
N	349	184		
Std. Dev.	1.94	1.12		
Encounters w/other park visitors				
Mean	0.76	0.78	0.14	0.89
N	348	183		
Std. Dev.	1.54	1.68		
Encounters w/groups of size >6				
Mean	0.04	0.03	-0.18	0.859
N	363	185		
Std. Dev.	0.01	0.02		
Encounters with NPS personnel				
Mean	0.04	0.01	-2.21	0.027
N	360	186		
Std. Dev.	0.19	0.10		
Seeing litter and human waste[2]				
% seeing	11.6%	10.5	0.51	0.698
N	370	190		

[1]The classification of near road was given to the first and last day of a hike, middle days of hikes that crossed the road, or in some cases if the hiker's map showed a route near the road; the category of away from road was assigned to all other days of the hike.
[2]Seeing litter and human waste was measured with a dichotomous variable, and, thus, a comparison of means is not appropriate. A chi-square test of association was conducted and reported.

Weather: To be included in the analysis, the following criteria were used with regard to the time period reported by respondents:

- The time period was entirely within the day (e.g., June 21, 8 a.m. to 4 p.m.; July 6, 12 a.m. to July 7 12 a.m. [interpreted as midnight July 6 to midnight July 7]; etc.).
- A time period that overlapped an evening ended at no later than 10 a.m. the following morning (e.g., August 15, 9 a.m. to August 16, 9 a.m.). However, in these cases the majority of the time block must have occurred on the first day (e.g., August 17 10 pm. To August 18 10 a.m., would not be included in the analysis).

When examining the level of indicators by weather, the only difference found was for motorized sound and seeing litter or human waste (Table 34). The difference in amount of motorized sound encountered could be due to fewer overflights during bad weather or perhaps rain and wind drowning out bus noise. It is not clear why seeing litter and human waste differed by weather. Perhaps people were more likely to be looking down during rainy weather, or perhaps those who hike in rainy weather are more sensitive to seeing litter and human waste.

Table 34. Influence of Weather on Indicators, Backpackers.

	Precipiation[1]			F / Welch	Sig.
	< = 0.2"	0.21 to 0.4"	> 0.4"		
Motorized sound encounters					
Mean[2]	3.40[a]	4.03[a]	1.69[b]	14.31[3]	< .001
N	265	38	64		
Std. Dev.	4.16	3.69	2.00		
Modern equipment encounters					
Mean	0.92	1.46	0.86	0.81	.447
N	269	39	65		
Std. Dev.	2.66	3.17	1.89		
Landscape modifications					
Mean	1.01	0.92	1.09	0.11	0.893
N	272	39	66		
Std. Dev.	1.33	1.18	3.16		
Encounters w/other park visitors					
Mean	0.74	0.64	0.37	2.22	0.11
N	271	39	68		
Std. Dev.	1.34	1.04	1.32		
Encounters w/groups of size >6					
Mean	0.04	0.00	0.00	--	--
N	276	39	69		
Std. Dev.	0.22	0.00	0.00		
Encounters with NPS personnel					
Mean	0.02	0.03	0.01	0.10	0.90
N	276	39	70		
Std. Dev.	0.15	0.16	0.12		
Seeing litter or human waste[4]					
% seeing	9.9%	2.6%	21.4%	10.70	0.005
N	282	39	70		

[1]Recorded at the Eielson Visitor Center. See explanation preceding table regarding criteria for including weather data.
[2]Means with different superscripts were significantly different at $p = 0.05$.
[3]Unequal variance, the Welch statistic is presented.
[4]Seeing litter and human waste was measured with a dichotomous variable, and, thus, a comparison of means is not appropriate. A chi-square test of association was conducted and reported.

Length of Time Period Reported: Backpackers recorded the level of the indicators throughout their trip. This includes time spent at camp. They were also instructed to fill out a separate page for each unit in which they hiked. Backpackers filled in the start time and end time on each page that indicators were recorded. There was high variation in the length of time reported as some units were just passed through for a few hours and the hike to reach the road on the last day tended to be short. To examine if length of time of the reporting period was related to the level of the indicators, the length of time was collapsed into five levels: 0 – 3 hours, 3.01 – 5 hours, 5.01 – 7 hours, 7.01 – 10 hours, and > 10 hours. Although the majority of responses fall in the > 10 hour category, these categories were chosen to give a relatively even distribution to the categories falling under 10 hours. The level of motorized sound and encounters with others differed by length of time reported (Table 35).

Table 35. Comparison of Indicators by Length of Period Reported, Backpackers.

	Length of time period reported for						
	0 – 3	3.01 - 5	5.01 - 7	7.01 - 10	>10	F / Welch	Sig.
Motorized sound encounters							
Mean[1]	1.74[a]	2.40[a]	2.69[ab]	3.40[ab]	3.61[b]	6.74[2]	< 0.001
n	46	58	48	53	288		
Std. Dev.	1.67	2.07	3.23	4.90	4.74		
Modern equipment encounters							
Mean	1.60	0.75	0.65	0.97	1.04	1.01[2]	0.407
n	48	57	49	58	286		
Std. Dev.	3.70	1.57	1.61	3.04	2.84		
Landscape modifications							
Mean	0.98	1.12	0.82	0.76	1.12	0.77	0.545
n	48	57	49	59	292		
Std. Dev.	1.31	1.02	1.09	0.84	2.10		
Encounters w/other park visitors							
Mean[1]	0.30[a]	0.42[a]	0.72[ab]	0.56[ab]	0.91[b]	5.33[2]	< 0.001
n	46	59	50	59	289		
Std. Dev.	0.66	0.70	1.03	0.97	1.77		
Encounters w/groups of size >6							
Mean	0.04	0.03	0.00	0.00	0.05	-[2]	-
n	49	59	50	61	297		
Std. Dev.	0.20	0.18	0.00	0.00	0.26		
Encounters with NPS personnel							
Mean	0.00	0.03	0.00	0.02	0.04	-[2]	-
n	49	59	49	60	297		
Std. Dev.	0.00	0.18	0.00	0.13	0.21		
Seeing litter or human waste[3]							
% seeing	8.2%	6.7%	10.0%	6.6%	13.0%	4.12	0.39
n	49	60	50	61	308		

[1]Means with different superscripts were different at p = .05.
[2]Unequal variance, the Welch statistic is presented. The Welch cannot be calculated for encounters with groups > 6 and NPS personnel as there was no variance in at least one group.
[3]Seeing litter or human waste was measured with a dichotomous variable, and, thus, a comparison of means is not appropriate. A chi-square test of association was conducted and reported.

Level of Indicators Reported as Zero Tolerance: This section evaluates the standards from an absolute perspective; if one person reports a level above the standard, the standard is violated. For this analysis, when examining results by unit, small sample sizes are not an issue when the standard is violated. However, caution should be used in generalizing results from units with small *n*s in which the standard was not violated.

Percent of Respondents for Which the Standards are Violated: The distribution of data for the levels of the indicators was collapsed into a category of not exceeding the standard and several categories above the standard. Data were analyzed for each of the 32 units in which backpackers hiked. Results show that for motorized sound and landscape modifications, there were few units that were not violating the standard.

- Motorized sound: five units did *not* violate the standard (Table 36).
- Modern equipment: 11 units did *not* violate the standard (Table 37).
- Landscape modifications: four units did *not* violate the standard (Table 38).
- Encounters with other park visitors: 20 units did *not* violate the standard (Table 39).
- Seeing Litter or Human Waste: 10 units did *not* violate the standard (see Table 31 on page 34).
- Encounters with groups larger than six and encounters with NPS rangers or researchers: no units violated the standard.

Table 36. Motorized Sound, Backpackers.

Unit	n	<= 1	2 – 5	6 – 10	>= 11	Percent above standard
3	1	0.0%	0.0%	100.0%	0.0%	100.0%
4	13	38.5%	38.5%	23.1%	0.0%	61.5%
5	18	5.6%	44.4%	38.9%	11.1%	94.4%
6	60	13.3%	70.0%	15.0%	1.7%	86.7%
7	15	20.0%	33.3%	26.7%	20.0%	80.0%
8	15	20.0%	53.3%	20.0%	6.7%	80.0%
9	46	41.3%	26.1%	28.3%	4.3%	58.7%
10	51	31.4%	47.1%	15.7%	5.9%	68.6%
11	15	46.7%	46.7%	6.7%	0.0%	53.3%
12	34	32.4%	55.9%	2.9%	8.8%	67.6%
13	34	23.5%	55.9%	11.8%	8.8%	76.5%
14	1	100.0%	0.0%	0.0%	0.0%	0.0%
15	7	85.7%	14.3%	0.0%	0.0%	14.3%
16	1	100.0%	0.0%	0.0%	0.0%	0.0%
18	23	56.5%	21.7%	17.4%	4.3%	43.5%
19	5	40.0%	60.0%	0.0%	0.0%	60.0%
24	2	50.0%	50.0%	0.0%	0.0%	50.0%
25	2	100.0%	0.0%	0.0%	0.0%	0.0%
26	18	55.6%	33.3%	5.6%	5.6%	44.4%
28	5	60.0%	20.0%	20.0%	0.0%	40.0%
29	11	18.2%	36.4%	45.5%	0.0%	81.8%
30	3	66.7%	33.3%	0.0%	0.0%	33.3%
31	25	56.0%	36.0%	8.0%	0.0%	44.0%
32	31	51.6%	41.9%	3.2%	3.2%	48.4%
33	27	74.1%	18.5%	7.4%	0.0%	25.9%
34	20	60.0%	40.0%	0.0%	0.0%	40.0%
35	9	77.8%	11.1%	11.1%	0.0%	22.2%
36	1	0.0%	100.0%	0.0%	0.0%	100.0%
38	3	33.3%	66.7%	0.0%	0.0%	66.7%
39	16	68.8%	31.3%	0.0%	0.0%	31.2%
41[1]	2	100.0%	0.0%	0.0%	0.0%	0.0%
42[1]	9	44.4%	55.6%	0.0%	0.0%	0.0%

[1]The motorized sound standard for units 41 and 42 is no more than 10 per day.

Table 37. Modern Equipment Distribution, Backpackers.

Unit	n	<= 1	2 – 5	6 – 10	> 10	Percent above standard
3	1	0.0%	100.0%	0.0%	0.0%	100.0%
4	15	93.3%	6.7%	0.0%	0.0%	6.7%
5	18	83.3%	16.7%	0.0%	0.0%	16.7%
6	60	91.7%	6.7%	1.7%	0.0%	8.3%
7	14	64.3%	28.6%	7.1%	0.0%	35.7%
8	16	62.5%	6.3%	25%	6.3%	37.5%
9	45	80.0%	6.7%	11.1%	2.2%	20.0%
10	50	72.0%	16.0%	8.0%	4.0%	28.0%
11	15	100.0%	0.0%	0.0%	0.0%	0.0%
12	34	88.2%	11.8%	0.0%	0.0%	11.8%
13	35	77.1%	20.0%	2.9%	0.0%	22.9%
14	1	100.0%	0.0%	0.0%	0.0%	0.0%
15	7	85.7%	0.0%	14.3%	0.0%	14.3%
16	1	100.0%	0.0%	0.0%	0.0%	0.0%
18	24	95.8%	0.0%	4.2%	0.0%	4.2%
19	6	83.3%	16.7%	0.0%	0.0%	16.7%
24	2	100.0%	0.0%	0.0%	0.0%	0.0%
25	2	100.0%	0.0%	0.0%	0.0%	0.0%
26	18	77.8%	11.1%	5.6%	5.6%	22.2%
28	5	60.0%	20.0%	20.0%	0.0%	40.0%
29	11	54.5%	36.4%	9.1%	0.0%	45.5%
30	3	100.0%	0.0%	0.0%	0.0%	0.0%
31	25	100.0%	0.0%	0.0%	0.0%	0.0%
32	29	82.8%	10.3%	3.4%	3.4%	17.2%
33	28	100.0%	0.0%	0.0%	0.0%	0.0%
34	21	90.5%	9.5%	0.0%	0.0%	9,5%
35	9	88.9%	11.1%	0.0%	0.0%	11.1%
36	1	0.0%	100.0%	0.0%	0.0%	100.0%
38	3	100.0%	0.0%	0.0%	0.0%	0.0%
39	15	100.0%	0.0%	0.0%	0.0%	0.0%
41	3	100.0%	0.0%	0.0%	0.0%	0.0%
42	9	66.7%	33.3%	0.0%	0.0%	33.3%

Table 38. Landscape Modification Distribution, Backpackers.

Unit	n	0	1 – 5	6 – 10	> 10	Percent above standard
3	2	0.0%	100.0%	0.0%	0.0%	100.0%
4	15	53.3%	46.7%	0.0%	0.0%	46.7%
5	19	68.4%	31.6%	0.0%	0.0%	31.6%
6	62	43.5%	53.2%	3.2%	0.0%	56.5%
7	15	26.7%	73.3%	0.0%	0.0%	73.3%
8	17	35.3%	58.8%	0.0%	5.9%	64.7%
9	46	41.3%	54.3%	4.3%	0.0%	58.7%
10	49	40.8%	59.2%	0.0%	0.0%	59.2%
11	15	33.3%	66.7%	0.0%	0.0%	66.7%
12	34	29.4%	70.6%	0.0%	0.0%	70.6%
13	35	28.6%	71.4%	0.0%	0.0%	71.4%
14	1	100.0%	0.0%	0.0%	0.0%	0.0%
15	7	71.4%	14.3%	14.3%	0.0%	28.6%
16	1	100.0%	0.0%	0.0%	0.0%	0.0%
18	24	62.5%	37.5%	0.0%	0.0%	37.5%
19	6	83.3%	16.7%	0.0%	0.0%	16.7%
24	2	50.0%	50.0%	0.0%	0.0%	50.0%
25	2	50.0%	50.0%	0.0%	0.0%	50.0%
26	18	16.7%	83.3%	0.0%	0.0%	83.3%
28	5	40.0%	60.0%	0.0%	0.0%	60.0%
29	11	9.1%	90.9%	0.0%	0.0%	90.9%
30	3	0.0%	100.0%	0.0%	0.0%	100.0%
31	25	28.0%	72.0%	0.0%	0.0%	72.0%
32	31	54.8%	41.9%	0.0%	3.2%	45.2%
33	28	85.7%	14.3%	0.0%	0.0%	14.3%
34	21	52.4%	47.6%	0.0%	0.0%	47.6%
35	9	66.7%	33.3%	0.0%	0.0%	33.3%
36	1	100.0%	0.0%	0.0%	0.0%	0.0%
38	3	100.0%	0.0%	0.0%	0.0%	0.0%
39	15	93.3%	6.7%	0.0%	0.0%	6.7%
41	3	0.0%	100.0%	0.0%	0.0%	100.0%
42	9	0.0%	100.0%	0.0%	0.0%	100.0%

Table 39. Encounters with Other Park Visitors, Backpackers.

Unit	n	0 - 2	3 – 5	6 – 10	> 10	Percent above standard
3	2	100.0%	0.0%	0.0%	0.0%	0.0%
4	15	100.0%	0.0%	0.0%	0.0%	0.0%
5	18	94.4%	5.6%	0.0%	0.0%	5.6%
6	61	91.8%	3.3%	3.3%	1.6%	8.2%
7	15	100.0%	0.0%	0.0%	0.0%	0.0%
8	18	88.9%	11.1%	0.0%	0.0%	11.1%
9	45	97.8%	2.2%	0.0%	0.0%	2.2%
10	51	84.3%	15.7%	0.0%	0.0%	15.7%
11	14	100.0%	0.0%	0.0%	0.0%	0.0%
12	35	88.6%	8.6%	2.9%	0.0%	11.4%
13	34	85.3%	14.7%	0.0%	0.0%	14.7%
14	1	100.0%	0.0%	0.0%	0.0%	0.0%
15	7	85.7%	14.3%	0.0%	0.0%	14.3%
16	1	100.0%	0.0%	0.0%	0.0%	0.0%
18	24	100.0%	0.0%	0.0%	0.0%	0.0%
19	6	83.3%	0.0%	16.7%	0.0%	16.7%
24	2	50.0%	0.0%	50.0%	0.0%	50.0%
25	2	100.0%	0.0%	0.0%	0.0%	0.0%
26	18	83.3%	11.1%	5.6%	0.0%	16.7%
28	5	100.0%	0.0%	0.0%	0.0%	0.0%
29	11	100.0%	0.0%	0.0%	0.0%	0.0%
30	3	100.0%	0.0%	0.0%	0.0%	0.0%
31	25	100.0%	0.0%	0.0%	0.0%	0.0%
32	31	100.0%	0.0%	0.0%	0.0%	0.0%
33	29	100.0%	0.0%	0.0%	0.0%	0.0%
34	21	100.0%	0.0%	0.0%	0.0%	0.0%
35	9	100.0%	0.0%	0.0%	0.0%	0.0%
36	1	100.0%	0.0%	0.0%	0.0%	0.0%
38	3	100.0%	0.0%	0.0%	0.0%	0.0%
39	15	100.0%	0.0%	0.0%	0.0%	0.0%
41	2	100.0%	0.0%	0.0%	0.0%	0.0%
42	9	77.8%	11.1%	0.0%	11.1%	22.2%

Percent of Days Standards are Violated: If a zero tolerance definition of when a standard is violated is adopted, the number of days in which a standard was violated can be calculated. For the backpackers a complicating factor is that the survey measured the indicators per 24 hour period (when applicable, i.e., no unit changes or completion of hike), rather than using a time period corresponding to a calendar day. respondents were instructed to essentially restart the recording period in the morning. However, people varied greatly in when they appeared to wake up and commence with that day's hike. The analysis in this section shows the percent of people who reported conditions above a standard for specific days. To be included in the analysis, the following criteria were used with regard to the time period reported by respondents:

- The time period was entirely within the day (e.g., June 21, 8 a.m. to 4 p.m.; July 6, 12 a.m. to July 7 12 a.m. [interpreted as midnight July 6 to midnight July 7]; etc.).

- A time period that overlapped an evening ended at no later than 10 a.m. the following morning (e.g., August 15, 9 a.m. to August 16, 9 a.m.). However, in these cases the majority of the time block must have occurred on the first day (e.g., August 17 10 pm. To August 18 10 a.m., would not be included in the analysis).

There were 87 different days in which respondents in the sample hiked.
- Motorized sound: 13 days did *not* violate the standard (Table 40).
- Modern equipment: 43 days did *not* violate the standard (Table 41).
- Landscape modifications: 6 days did *not* violate the standards (Table 42).
- Encounters with other park visitors: 66 days did *not* violate the standard (Table 43).
- Seeing litter or human waste: 50 days did *not* violate the standard (Table 44).
- Camping out of sight or sound of others: the 31 reports of not being able to camp out of sight or sound of others occurred on 25 different days (Table 45).

Table 40. Percent of Backpackers Reporting the Motorized Sound Standard was Violated, by Day[1].

Date	% > 1	n	Date	% > 1	n	Date	% > 1	n
31-May-10	100.0	1	1-Jul-10	25.0	4	1-Aug-10	100.0	1
1-Jun-10	100.0	1	2-Jul-10	75.0	8	2-Aug-10	100.0	1
3-Jun-10	0.0	1	3-Jul-10	50.0	2	3-Aug-10	100.0	3
4-Jun-10	66.7	3	4-Jul-10	66.7	3	4-Aug-10	0.0	3
5-Jun-10	0.0	1	5-Jul-10	50.0	6	5-Aug-10	50.0	4
7-Jun-10	100.0	1	6-Jul-10	85.7	7	6-Aug-10	60.0	5
10-Jun-10	66.7	3	7-Jul-10	71.4	7	7-Aug-10	66.7	6
11-Jun-10	0.0	2	8-Jul-10	71.4	7	8-Aug-10	88.9	9
12-Jun-10	0.0	2	9-Jul-10	0.0	3	9-Aug-10	80.0	5
13-Jun-10	83.3	6	10-Jul-10	14.3	7	10-Aug-10	50.0	2
14-Jun-10	75.0	4	11-Jul-10	0.0	5	11-Aug-10	71.4	7
15-Jun-10	60.0	5	12-Jul-10	50.0	10	12-Aug-10	60.0	10
16-Jun-10	66.7	3	13-Jul-10	50.0	12	13-Aug-10	42.9	7
17-Jun-10	100.0	2	14-Jul-10	42.9	7	14-Aug-10	57.1	7
18-Jun-10	50.0	4	15-Jul-10	33.3	3	15-Aug-10	0.0	4
19-Jun-10	100.0	6	16-Jul-10	100.0	2	16-Aug-10	25.0	4
20-Jun-10	66.7	6	17-Jul-10	71.4	7	17-Aug-10	0.0	2
21-Jun-10	69.2	13	18-Jul-10	85.7	7	18-Aug-10	66.7	3
22-Jun-10	77.8	9	19-Jul-10	66.7	3	19-Aug-10	75.0	4
23-Jun-10	61.5	13	20-Jul-10	50.0	6	20-Aug-10	0.0	1
24-Jun-10	45.5	11	21-Jul-10	33.3	3	22-Aug-10	0.0	1
25-Jun-10	50.0	10	22-Jul-10	100.0	2	23-Aug-10	0.0	1
26-Jun-10	40.0	5	23-Jul-10	80.0	5	24-Aug-10	100.0	1
27-Jun-10	80.0	5	24-Jul-10	100.0	4	25-Aug-10	66.7	3
28-Jun-10	83.3	6	25-Jul-10	100.0	3	26-Aug-10	33.3	3
29-Jun-10	88.9	9	26-Jul-10	100.0	3	27-Aug-10	60.0	5
30-Jun-10	60.0	5	27-Jul-10	66.7	6	28-Aug-10	50.0	6
			28-Jul-10	80.0	5	29-Aug-10	66.7	3
			29-Jul-10	60.0	5			
			30-Jul-10	0.0	2			
			31-Jul-10	100.0	2			

[1]Units 41 and 42 had a different standard for motorized sound violation (no more than 10 per day). There were 12 days in which backpackers reported for units 41 and 42. None of those days were over the standard.

Table 41. Percent of Backpackers Reporting the Modern Equipment Standard was Violated, by Day.

Date	% > 1	n	Date	% > 1	n	Date	% > 1	n
31-May-10	0.0	1	1-Jul-10	0.0	4	1-Aug-10	0.0	1
1-Jun-10	100.0	1	2-Jul-10	14.3	7	2-Aug-10	0.0	1
3-Jun-10	0.0	1	3-Jul-10	33.3	3	3-Aug-10	33.3	3
4-Jun-10	0.0	2	4-Jul-10	0.0	3	4-Aug-10	33.3	3
5-Jun-10	100.0	1	5-Jul-10	33.3	6	5-Aug-10	25.0	4
7-Jun-10	0.0	1	6-Jul-10	57.1	7	6-Aug-10	0.0	7
8-Jun-10	0.0	1	7-Jul-10	14.3	7	7-Aug-10	14.3	7
10-Jun-10	33.3	3	8-Jul-10	0.0	7	8-Aug-10	10.0	10
11-Jun-10	0.0	2	9-Jul-10	33.3	3	9-Aug-10	16.7	6
12-Jun-10	0.0	2	10-Jul-10	0.0	7	10-Aug-10	50.0	2
13-Jun-10	0.0	6	11-Jul-10	0.0	5	11-Aug-10	0.0	7
14-Jun-10	0.0	4	12-Jul-10	0.0	10	12-Aug-10	0.0	10
15-Jun-10	0.0	5	13-Jul-10	25.0	12	13-Aug-10	0.0	7
16-Jun-10	0.0	3	14-Jul-10	14.3	7	14-Aug-10	28.6	7
17-Jun-10	0.0	2	15-Jul-10	0.0	3	15-Aug-10	0.0	4
18-Jun-10	25.0	4	16-Jul-10	0.0	3	16-Aug-10	25.0	4
19-Jun-10	16.7	6	17-Jul-10	14.3	7	17-Aug-10	0.0	2
20-Jun-10	33.3	6	18-Jul-10	12.5	8	18-Aug-10	0.0	3
21-Jun-10	33.3	12	19-Jul-10	0.0	3	19-Aug-10	0.0	4
22-Jun-10	22.2	9	20-Jul-10	0.0	7	20-Aug-10	0.0	1
23-Jun-10	23.1	13	21-Jul-10	20.0	5	22-Aug-10	0.0	1
24-Jun-10	9.1	11	22-Jul-10	33.3	3	23-Aug-10	0.0	1
25-Jun-10	10.0	10	23-Jul-10	14.3	7	24-Aug-10	0.0	1
26-Jun-10	0.0	5	24-Jul-10	20.0	5	25-Aug-10	0.0	3
27-Jun-10	20.0	5	25-Jul-10	50.0	4	26-Aug-10	0.0	3
28-Jun-10	16.7	6	26-Jul-10	0.0	2	27-Aug-10	0.0	5
29-Jun-10	22.2	9	27-Jul-10	14.3	7	28-Aug-10	33.3	6
30-Jun-10	40.0	5	28-Jul-10	16.7	6	29-Aug-10	33.3	3
			29-Jul-10	0.0	6			
			30-Jul-10	0.0	2			
			31-Jul-10	50.0	2			

Table 42. Percent of Backpackers Reporting the Landscape Modification Standard was Violated, by Day.

Date	% > 0	n	Date	% > 0	n	Date	% > 0	n
31-May-10	100.0	1	1-Jul-10	40.0	5	1-Aug-10	100.0	1
1-Jun-10	100.0	1	2-Jul-10	62.5	8	2-Aug-10	100.0	1
3-Jun-10	100.0	1	3-Jul-10	33.3	3	3-Aug-10	100.0	3
4-Jun-10	100.0	2	4-Jul-10	66.7	3	4-Aug-10	66.7	3
5-Jun-10	100.0	1	5-Jul-10	83.3	6	5-Aug-10	25.0	4
7-Jun-10	100.0	1	6-Jul-10	71.4	7	6-Aug-10	42.9	7
8-Jun-10	100.0	1	7-Jul-10	71.4	7	7-Aug-10	42.9	7
10-Jun-10	66.7	3	8-Jul-10	28.6	7	8-Aug-10	50.0	10
11-Jun-10	50.0	2	9-Jul-10	0.0	3	9-Aug-10	50.0	6
12-Jun-10	50.0	2	10-Jul-10	42.9	7	10-Aug-10	100.0	3
13-Jun-10	50.0	6	11-Jul-10	66.7	6	11-Aug-10	71.4	7
14-Jun-10	50.0	4	12-Jul-10	30.0	10	12-Aug-10	50.0	10
15-Jun-10	60.0	5	13-Jul-10	58.3	12	13-Aug-10	71.4	7
16-Jun-10	100.0	3	14-Jul-10	57.1	7	14-Aug-10	71.4	7
17-Jun-10	50.0	2	15-Jul-10	33.3	3	15-Aug-10	0.0	4
18-Jun-10	50.0	4	16-Jul-10	66.7	3	16-Aug-10	50.0	4
19-Jun-10	66.7	6	17-Jul-10	57.1	7	17-Aug-10	50.0	2
20-Jun-10	33.3	6	18-Jul-10	50.0	8	18-Aug-10	66.7	3
21-Jun-10	61.5	13	19-Jul-10	66.7	3	19-Aug-10	50.0	4
22-Jun-10	62.5	8	20-Jul-10	57.1	7	20-Aug-10	0.0	1
23-Jun-10	46.2	13	21-Jul-10	100.0	5	22-Aug-10	0.0	1
24-Jun-10	63.6	11	22-Jul-10	66.7	3	23-Aug-10	0.0	1
25-Jun-10	50.0	10	23-Jul-10	71.4	7	24-Aug-10	50.0	2
26-Jun-10	0.0	5	24-Jul-10	60.0	5	25-Aug-10	33.3	3
27-Jun-10	20.0	5	25-Jul-10	50.0	4	26-Aug-10	66.7	3
28-Jun-10	33.3	6	26-Jul-10	100.0	3	27-Aug-10	40.0	5
29-Jun-10	55.6	9	27-Jul-10	100.0	7	28-Aug-10	33.3	6
30-Jun-10	60.0	5	28-Jul-10	66.7	6	29-Aug-10	33.3	3
			29-Jul-10	66.7	6			
			30-Jul-10	50.0	2			
			31-Jul-10	50.0	2			

Table 43. Percent of Backpackers Reporting the Encounters with Other Visitors Standard was Violated, by Day.

Date	% > 2	n	Date	% > 2	n	Date	% > 2	n
31-May-10	0.0	1	1-Jul-10	0.0	5	1-Aug-10	100.0	1
1-Jun-10	0.0	1	2-Jul-10	22.2	9	2-Aug-10	0.0	1
3-Jun-10	0.0	1	3-Jul-10	0.0	4	3-Aug-10	0.0	3
4-Jun-10	0.0	2	4-Jul-10	0.0	3	4-Aug-10	0.0	2
5-Jun-10	0.0	1	5-Jul-10	16.7	6	5-Aug-10	0.0	4
7-Jun-10	0.0	1	6-Jul-10	0.0	7	6-Aug-10	0.0	7
8-Jun-10	0.0	1	7-Jul-10	0.0	7	7-Aug-10	0.0	7
10-Jun-10	33.3	3	8-Jul-10	14.3	7	8-Aug-10	0.0	10
11-Jun-10	50.0	2	9-Jul-10	0.0	3	9-Aug-10	0.0	6
12-Jun-10	0.0	2	10-Jul-10	14.3	7	10-Aug-10	0.0	2
13-Jun-10	0.0	6	11-Jul-10	0.0	6	11-Aug-10	0.0	7
14-Jun-10	0.0	4	12-Jul-10	10.0	10	12-Aug-10	0.0	9
15-Jun-10	0.0	5	13-Jul-10	0.0	12	13-Aug-10	14.3	7
16-Jun-10	0.0	3	14-Jul-10	0.0	7	14-Aug-10	14.3	7
17-Jun-10	0.0	2	15-Jul-10	0.0	3	15-Aug-10	0.0	4
18-Jun-10	0.0	4	16-Jul-10	0.0	3	16-Aug-10	0.0	4
19-Jun-10	0.0	6	17-Jul-10	0.0	7	17-Aug-10	0.0	2
20-Jun-10	16.7	6	18-Jul-10	0.0	8	18-Aug-10	0.0	3
21-Jun-10	15.4	13	19-Jul-10	0.0	3	19-Aug-10	0.0	4
22-Jun-10	22.2	9	20-Jul-10	14.3	7	20-Aug-10	0.0	1
23-Jun-10	7.7	13	21-Jul-10	20.0	5	22-Aug-10	0.0	1
24-Jun-10	0.0	11	22-Jul-10	0.0	3	23-Aug-10	0.0	1
25-Jun-10	0.0	10	23-Jul-10	28.6	7	24-Aug-10	0.0	2
26-Jun-10	0.0	5	24-Jul-10	0.0	5	25-Aug-10	0.0	3
27-Jun-10	0.0	5	25-Jul-10	0.0	3	26-Aug-10	0.0	3
28-Jun-10	16.7	6	26-Jul-10	0.0	3	27-Aug-10	0.0	5
29-Jun-10	0.0	9	27-Jul-10	14.3	7	28-Aug-10	0.0	6
30-Jun-10	0.0	6	28-Jul-10	0.0	6	29-Aug-10	33.3	3
			29-Jul-10	0.0	6			
			30-Jul-10	0.0	2			
			31-Jul-10	50.0	2			

Table 44. Percent of Backpackers Reporting Seeing Litter or Human Waste, by Day.

Date	% seeing	n	Date	% seeing	n	Date	% seeing	n
31-May-10	0.0	1	1-Jul-10	0.0	5	1-Aug-10	0.0	1
1-Jun-10	0.0	1	2-Jul-10	11.1	9	2-Aug-10	0.0	1
3-Jun-10	0.0	1	3-Jul-10	25.0	4	3-Aug-10	25.0	4
4-Jun-10	0.0	3	4-Jul-10	33.3	3	4-Aug-10	0.0	3
5-Jun-10	0.0	1	5-Jul-10	16.7	6	5-Aug-10	25.0	4
6-Jun-10[1]	0.0	1	6-Jul-10	0.0	7	6-Aug-10	0.0	7
7-Jun-10	0.0	1	7-Jul-10	0.0	7	7-Aug-10	0.0	7
8-Jun-10	0.0	1	8-Jul-10	0.0	7	8-Aug-10	0.0	10
10-Jun-10	33.3	3	9-Jul-10	0.0	4	9-Aug-10	14.3	7
11-Jun-10	0.0	2	10-Jul-10	14.3	7	10-Aug-10	0.0	4
12-Jun-10	0.0	2	11-Jul-10	16.7	6	11-Aug-10	0.0	8
13-Jun-10	16.7	6	12-Jul-10	10.0	10	12-Aug-10	20.0	10
14-Jun-10	25.0	4	13-Jul-10	8.3	12	13-Aug-10	14.3	7
15-Jun-10	20.0	5	14-Jul-10	0.0	7	14-Aug-10	0.0	7
16-Jun-10	33.3	3	15-Jul-10	0.0	3	15-Aug-10	0.0	4
17-Jun-10	0.0	3	16-Jul-10	33.3	3	16-Aug-10	0.0	4
18-Jun-10	50.0	4	17-Jul-10	28.6	7	17-Aug-10	0.0	2
19-Jun-10	33.3	6	18-Jul-10	0.0	8	18-Aug-10	33.3	3
20-Jun-10	0.0	6	19-Jul-10	33.3	3	19-Aug-10	0.0	4
21-Jun-10	15.4	13	20-Jul-10	14.3	7	20-Aug-10	0.0	1
22-Jun-10	0.0	9	21-Jul-10	0.0	5	22-Aug-10	0.0	1
23-Jun-10	7.7	13	22-Jul-10	0.0	4	23-Aug-10	0.0	1
24-Jun-10	18.2	11	23-Jul-10	0.0	7	24-Aug-10	0.0	2
25-Jun-10	10.0	10	24-Jul-10	0.0	5	25-Aug-10	0.0	3
26-Jun-10	33.3	6	25-Jul-10	0.0	4	26-Aug-10	33.3	3
27-Jun-10	80.0	5	26-Jul-10	0.0	3	27-Aug-10	0.0	5
28-Jun-10	0.0	7	27-Jul-10	14.3	7	28-Aug-10	33.3	6
29-Jun-10	10.0	10	28-Jul-10	16.7	6	29-Aug-10	33.3	3
30-Jun-10	14.3	7	29-Jul-10	0.0	6			
			30-Jul-10	0.0	2			
			31-Jul-10	0.0	2			

[1]Due to item non-response June 6 does not show up in the tables for the other indicators.

Table 45. Dates in Which Respondents did not Camp Out of Sight or Sound of Others.

Date[1]	Unit	Date	Unit
15-Jun-10	29	31-Jul-10	6
16-Jun-10	29	2-Aug-10	3
22-Jun-10	9	3-Aug-10[2]	
26-Jun-10	35	7-Aug-10	42
28-Jun-10	8	7-Aug-10	7
30-Jun-10	6	8-Aug-10	33
1-Jul-10	10	8-Aug-10	33
9-Jul-10	29	8-Aug-10	6
11-Jul-10	31	11-Aug-10	34
12-Jul-10	31	11-Aug-10	9
13-Jul-10	33	12-Aug-10	9
13-Jul-10	39	13-Aug-10	9
20-Jul-10	31	13-Aug-10	12
25-Jul-10	8	19-Aug-10	8
26-Jul-10	8	24-Aug-10	8
28-Jul-10	12		

[1]The date refers to the first night of camping, e.g., if someone camped on the night of the June 15th to the morning of June 16, June 15 is listed. Two dates associated with not being able to camp out of sight or sound of others reported in the survey reflected a report made in the am; the date was changed to reflect the previous evening.

[2]August 3rd was marked by a respondent as not being able to camp out of sight or sound, however, a unit was not listed.

Percent of Time Encountering Indicators: Respondents were asked what percent of time they encountered motorized sound, landscape modifications, modern equipment and other park visitors. Response categories were 0 – 24%, 25 – 49%, 50 – 74%, and 75 – 100%. In general, visitors encountered the indicators less than 24% of the time (Table 46 – Table 49). Some exceptions were units with very low number of responses (e.g., encountering other visitors, unit 24 with an n of 3). However, other exceptions might indicate problem areas, e.g., motorized sound in unit 9 with an n of 46.

Table 46. Percent of Time Backpackers Heard Motorized Sound per Day, by Unit.

Unit	n	0%[1]	1 – 24%	25 – 49%	50 – 74%	75 – 100%
3	2	0.0%	0.0%	50.0%	50.0%	0.0%
4	15	20.0%	66.7%	13.3%	0.0%	0.0%
5	19	0.0%	84.2%	10.5%	5.3%	0.0%
6	62	4.8%	87.1%	8.1%	0.0%	0.0%
7	16	18.8%	50.0%	18.8%	12.5%	0.0%
8	20	15.0%	70.0%	5.0%	10.0%	0.0%
9	46	19.6%	69.6%	6.5%	4.3%	0.0%
10	51	19.6%	68.6%	9.8%	2.0%	0.0%
11	15	26.7%	60.0%	13.3%	0.0%	0.0%
12	38	15.8%	73.7%	5.3%	5.3%	0.0%
13	33	9.1%	81.8%	3.0%	6.1%	0.0%
15	7	57.1%	42.9%	0.0%	0.0%	0.0%
16	1	0.0%	100.0%	0.0%	0.0%	0.0%
18	23	21.7%	78.3%	0.0%	0.0%	0.0%
19	4	0.0%	100.0%	0.0%	0.0%	0.0%
24	3	33.3%	0.0%	66.7%	0.0%	0.0%
25	2	100.0%	0.0%	0.0%	0.0%	0.0%
26	17	47.1%	41.2%	5.9%	5.9%	0.0%
28	5	40.0%	60.0%	0.0%	0.0%	0.0%
29	12	0.0%	100.0%	0.0%	0.0%	0.0%
30	3	33.3%	66.7%	0.0%	0.0%	0.0%
31	26	30.8%	69.2%	0.0%	0.0%	0.0%
32	31	16.1%	67.7%	12.9%	3.2%	0.0%
33	31	35.5%	58.1%	6.5%	0.0%	0.0%
34	23	43.5%	56.5%	0.0%	0.0%	0.0%
35	9	77.8%	11.1%	11.1%	0.0%	0.0%
36	2	0.0%	100.0%	0.0%	0.0%	0.0%
38	3	33.3%	66.7%	0.0%	0.0%	0.0%
39	16	25.0%	75.0%	0.0%	0.0%	0.0%
41	3	66.7%	33.3%	0.0%	0.0%	0.0%
42	9	44.4%	44.4%	11.1%	0.0%	0.0%

[1]On the survey the lowest response category was 0 – 24%. The 0% category was created from those who reported they did not hear any motorized sounds.

Table 47. Percent of Time Backpackers Saw Modern Equipment per Day, by Unit.

Unit	n	0%[1]	1 – 24%	25 – 49%	50 – 74%	75 – 100%
3	2	0.0%	0.0%	100.0%	0.0%	0.0%
4	15	73.3%	26.7%	0.0%	0.0%	0.0%
5	19	73.7%	21.1%	5.3%	0.0%	0.0%
6	60	83.3%	13.3%	1.7%	1.7%	0.0%
7	16	56.3%	37.5%	0.0%	6.3%	0.0%
8	20	35.0%	50.0%	10.0%	5.0%	0.0%
9	47	63.8%	29.8%	2.1%	4.3%	0.0%
10	50	60.0%	24.0%	10.0%	2.0%	4.0%
11	15	100.0%	0.0%	0.0%	0.0%	0.0%
12	38	60.5%	18.4%	0.0%	18.4%	2.6%
13	33	60.6%	27.3%	6.1%	3.0%	3.0%
15	7	85.7%	0.0%	14.3%	0.0%	0.0%
16	1	100.0%	0.0%	0.0%	0.0%	0.0%
18	22	90.9%	9.1%	0.0%	0.0%	0.0%
19	4	50.0%	50.0%	0.0%	0.0%	0.0%
24	3	33.3%	33.3%	33.3%	0.0%	0.0%
25	2	100.0%	0.0%	0.0%	0.0%	0.0%
26	18	66.7%	11.1%	5.6%	5.6%	11.1%
28	5	60.0%	20.0%	20.0%	0.0%	0.0%
29	12	50.0%	41.7%	8.3%	0.0%	0.0%
30	3	100.0%	0.0%	0.0%	0.0%	0.0%
31	25	84.0%	16.0%	0.0%	0.0%	0.0%
32	31	45.2%	25.8%	16.1%	12.9%	0.0%
33	30	83.3%	13.3%	3.3%	0.0%	0.0%
34	22	54.5%	36.4%	0.0%	0.0%	9.1%
35	9	66.7%	22.2%	11.1%	0.0%	0.0%
36	2	0.0%	100.0%	0.0%	0.0%	0.0%
38	3	100.0%	0.0%	0.0%	0.0%	0.0%
39	15	93.3%	6.7%	0.0%	0.0%	0.0%
41	3	100.0%	0.0%	0.0%	0.0%	0.0%
42	9	33.3%	66.7%	0.0%	0.0%	0.0%

[1]On the survey the lowest response category was 0 – 24%. The 0% category was created from those who reported they did not see any modern equipment.

Table 48. Percent of Time Backpackers Saw Landscape Modifications per Day, by Unit.

Unit	n	0%[1]	1 – 24%	25 – 49%	50 – 74%	75 – 100%
3	2	0.0%	50.0%	50.0%	0.0%	0.0%
4	15	53.3%	33.3%	6.7%	6.7%	0.0%
5	19	68.4%	26.3%	5.3%	0.0%	0.0%
6	62	41.9%	43.5%	12.9%	0.0%	1.6%
7	15	20.0%	66.7%	6.7%	6.7%	0.0%
8	20	30.0%	40.0%	10.0%	0.0%	20.0%
9	46	41.3%	52.2%	2.2%	0.0%	4.3%
10	50	38.0%	38.0%	10.0%	10.0%	4.0%
11	14	35.7%	50.0%	0.0%	14.3%	0.0%
12	37	27.0%	48.6%	2.7%	16.2%	5.4%
13	32	28.1%	34.4%	28.1%	6.3%	3.1%
15	7	71.4%	14.3%	14.3%	0.0%	0.0%
16	1	100.0%	0.0%	0.0%	0.0%	0.0%
18	22	59.1%	18.2%	22.7%	0.0%	0.0%
19	4	75.0%	25.0%	0.0%	0.0%	0.0%
24	3	33.3%	0.0%	33.3%	0.0%	33.3%
25	2	50.0%	50.0%	0.0%	0.0%	0.0%
26	18	16.7%	16.7%	16.7%	27.8%	22.2%
28	5	40.0%	60.0%	0.0%	0.0%	0.0%
29	12	8.3%	50.0%	8.3%	8.3%	25.0%
30	3	0.0%	100.0%	0.0%	0.0%	0.0%
31	25	24.0%	68.0%	8.0%	0.0%	0.0%
32	31	51.6%	29.0%	19.4%	0.0%	0.0%
33	30	76.7%	20.0%	3.3%	0.0%	0.0%
34	22	45.5%	54.5%	0.0%	0.0%	0.0%
35	9	66.7%	22.2%	11.1%	0.0%	0.0%
36	2	50.0%	0.0%	50.0%	0.0%	0.0%
38	3	100.0%	0.0%	0.0%	0.0%	0.0%
39	15	86.7%	13.3%	0.0%	0.0%	0.0%
41	3	0.0%	0.0%	0.0%	33.3%	66.7%
42	9	0.0%	44.4%	0.0%	0.0%	55.6%

[1]On the survey the lowest response category was 0 – 24%. The 0% category was created from those who reported they did not see any landscape modifications.

Table 49. Percent of Time Backpackers Saw other Park Visitors per Day, by Unit.

Unit	n	0%[1]	1 – 24%	25 – 49%	50 – 74%	75 – 100%
3	2	100.0%	0.0%	0.0%	0.0%	0.0%
4	15	73.3%	26.7%	0.0%	0.0%	0.0%
5	19	78.9%	21.1%	0.0%	0.0%	0.0%
6	62	53.2%	43.5%	1.6%	1.6%	0.0%
7	16	81.3%	18.8%	0.0%	0.0%	0.0%
8	19	31.6%	63.2%	5.3%	0.0%	0.0%
9	46	50.0%	43.5%	6.5%	0.0%	0.0%
10	51	35.3%	64.7%	0.0%	0.0%	0.0%
11	15	60.0%	40.0%	0.0%	0.0%	0.0%
12	37	56.8%	35.1%	5.4%	2.7%	0.0%
13	33	51.5%	39.4%	9.1%	0.0%	0.0%
15	7	42.9%	42.9%	14.3%	0.0%	0.0%
16	1	100.0%	0.0%	0.0%	0.0%	0.0%
18	23	69.6%	30.4%	0.0%	0.0%	0.0%
19	4	75.0%	25.0%	0.0%	0.0%	0.0%
24	3	33.3%	33.3%	33.3%	0.0%	0.0%
25	2	100.0%	0.0%	0.0%	0.0%	0.0%
26	18	44.4%	55.6%	0.0%	0.0%	0.0%
28	5	100.0%	0.0%	0.0%	0.0%	0.0%
29	12	50.0%	50.0%	0.0%	0.0%	0.0%
30	3	66.7%	33.3%	0.0%	0.0%	0.0%
31	25	56.0%	44.0%	0.0%	0.0%	0.0%
32	31	67.7%	32.3%	0.0%	0.0%	0.0%
33	29	44.8%	44.8%	3.4%	3.4%	3.4%
34	20	55.0%	40.0%	0.0%	5.0%	0.0%
35	9	88.9%	11.1%	0.0%	0.0%	0.0%
36	2	50.0%	50.0%	0.0%	0.0%	0.0%
38	3	100.0%	0.0%	0.0%	0.0%	0.0%
39	15	60.0%	40.0%	0.0%	0.0%	0.0%
41	3	33.3%	66.7%	0.0%	0.0%	0.0%
42	9	33.3%	66.7%	0.0%	0.0%	0.0%

[1]On the survey the lowest response category was 0 – 24%. The 0% category was created from those who reported they did not see any other park visitors.

Day Hikers

Overall, for day hikers the standards for motorized sound, encounters with modern equipment, landscape modifications, and encounters with other park visitors had mean levels that exceeded the standards, and seeing litter and human waste had a level of respondents reporting that exceeded the standard (Table 50).

Table 50. Overall Mean Level of Indicators for Day Hikers.

	n	Mean	Median	Max	Standard Deviation	Lower 95% CI	Upper 95% CI
Motorized sound[1]	388	3.18	2.00	50	5.710	2.61	3.74
Equipment encounters	390	2.02	.00	75	6.424	1.38	2.66
Landscape modifications	382	1.94	1.00	60	4.312	1.51	2.37
Other park visitors	394	5.88	2.00	100	10.631	4.83	6.93
Number of groups > 6	432	0.68	.00	25	1.917	0.50	0.86
Encounters with NPS	438	0.60	.00	15	1.145	0.50	0.71
The indicators below are expressed as a percentage rather than a mean							
See litter/human waste	441	14.1			n/a	11.3	16.7

[1]Includes August 24 & 25, in which there was a search and rescue operation; the responses for those dates are: Aug 24, 0 1x; Aug 25 0 2x, 2 2x, 5 1x.

Mean Levels of / Percent Reporting Indicators by Unit: Results for the indicators are presented by unit. As noted in the discussion for each table, units with low sample sizes have low statistical power to detect differences.

Motorized Sound: standard = no more than one per day.
- Examining units with n $\geq$ 10 (n = 11), reveals 7 units with 95% confidence intervals (CI) of the means above one.
- However, for the three units with n $\geq$ 10 and 95% CIs that overlap one, statistical power is low (of these, unit 25 has the highest power of .61), and, thus, there is a high probability of incorrectly concluding the standard is not violated.

Table 51. Mean Level of Motorized Sound Reported by Day Hikers, by Unit.

Unit	n	Mean	Median	Max	SD	95% CI lower	95% CI upper
1	6	3.33	1	15	5.82	-1.32	7.99
2	1	3.00	3	3	-	-	-
3	1	2.00	2	2	-	-	-
4	5	1.60	1	5	2.07	-0.22	3.42
5	2	1.00	1	2	1.41	-0.96	2.96
6	17	5.65	4	20	6.59	2.51	8.78
7	3	2.33	3	3	1.15	1.03	3.64
8	11	3.27	2	15	4.17	0.81	5.74
9	9	3.56	5	6	2.24	2.09	5.02
10	5	3.00	2	10	4.12	-0.61	6.61
11	31	3.65	2	21	4.72	1.99	5.31
12	46	3.07	1	40	6.67	1.14	4.99
13	5	5.80	1	27	11.86	-4.60	16.20
14	7	1.71	1	6	2.06	0.19	3.24
15	3	2.33	2	3	0.58	1.68	2.99
20	1	1.00	1	1	-	-	-
24	29	7.28	2	50	13.91	2.21	12.34
25	40	1.73	1	10	2.35	1.00	2.45
26	7	2.14	2	5	1.86	0.76	3.52
27	1	4.00	4	4	-	-	-
28	5	2.40	1	9	3.78	-0.91	5.71
29	23	1.65	0	6	1.94	0.86	2.45
30	6	1.50	1	4	1.64	0.19	2.81
31	24	3.33	2	20	4.60	1.49	5.17
32	11	3.82	1	20	6.01	0.26	7.37
33	67	2.60	2	10	2.80	1.93	3.27
34	13	2.54	2	8	2.70	1.07	4.00
36	1	2.00	2	2	-	-	-

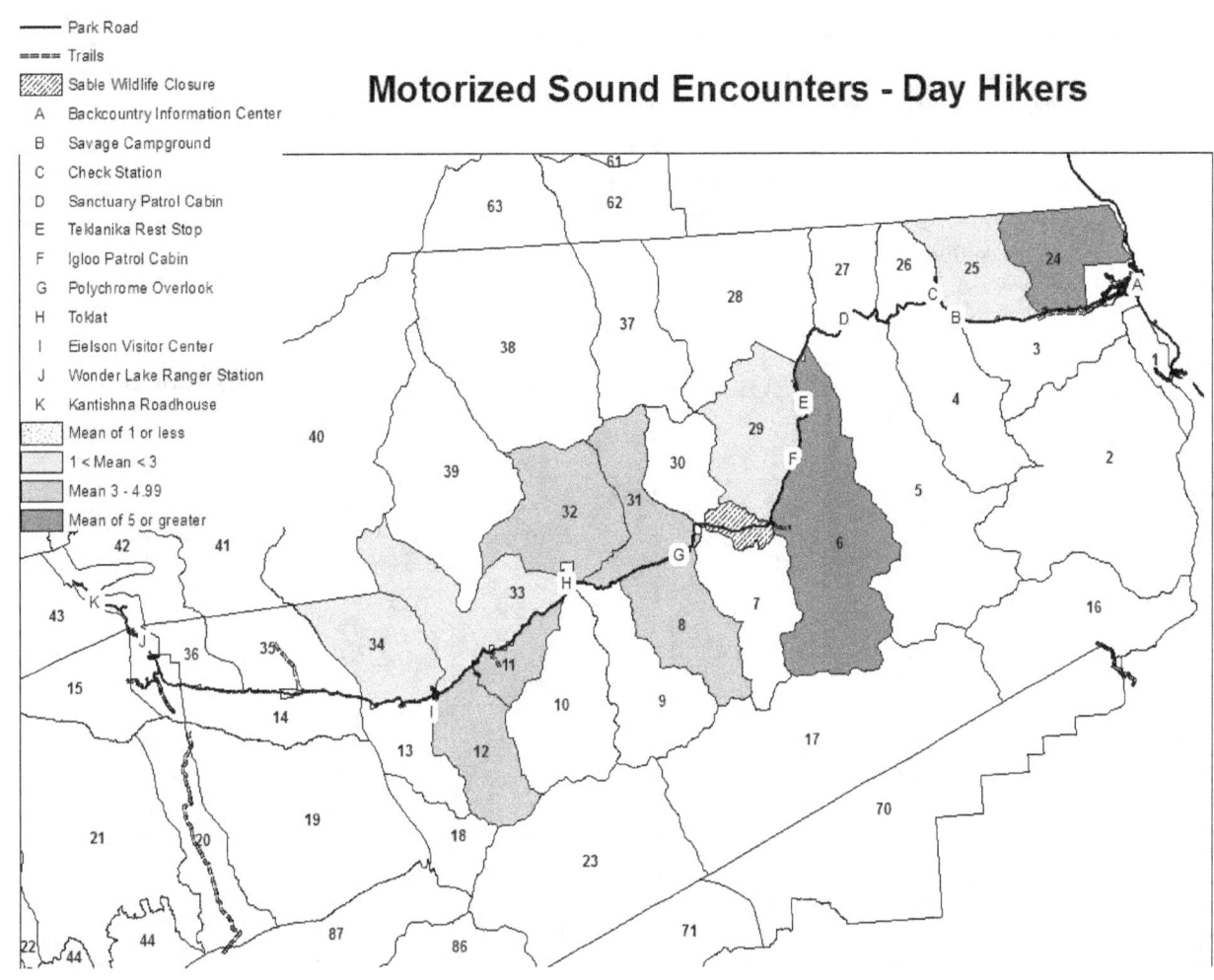

Figure 10. Distribution of Mean Level of Motorized Sound as Reported by Day Hikers, for Units with n > = 10.

Modern Equipment: standard = no more than one per day.
- Examining units with n > = 10 (n = 12), reveals no units with 95% confidence intervals (CI) of the mean above one, but 11 that overlap one.
- However, for the 11 units with n > = 10 and 95% CIs that overlap one, statistical power is low (due to high standard deviations in some cases and low ns in other cases), and, thus, there is a high probability of incorrectly concluding the standard is not violated.

Table 52. Mean Level of Encounters with Modern Equipment Reported by Day Hikers, by Unit.

Unit	n	Mean	Median	Max	*SD*	95% CI lower	95% CI upper
1	6	0.83	1	2	0.98	0.05	1.62
2	1	2.00	2	2	-	-	-
3	1	2.00	2	2	-	-	-
4	5	0.80	0	3	1.30	-0.34	1.94
5	2	0.50	1	1	0.71	-0.48	1.48
6	17	4.65	0	49	11.90	-1.01	10.30
7	3	0.33	0	1	0.58	-0.32	0.99
8	11	5.18	1	40	11.74	-1.75	12.12
9	10	1.20	0	5	2.10	-0.10	2.50
10	5	0.00	0	0	0.00	0.00	0.00
11	31	2.16	0	25	5.11	0.36	3.96
12	52	1.21	0	12	2.32	0.58	1.84
13	5	3.80	3	10	4.27	0.06	7.54
14	7	1.29	0	5	2.21	-0.35	2.93
15	3	1.33	0	4	2.31	-1.28	3.95
20	1	3.00	3	3	-	-	-
24	27	3.44	1	40	8.77	0.14	6.75
25	42	0.71	0	5	1.24	0.34	1.09
26	7	1.14	0	5	1.86	-0.24	2.52
27	1	4.00	4	4	-	-	-
28	5	0.80	0	3	1.30	-0.34	1.94
29	23	0.57	0	2	0.84	0.22	0.91
30	6	1.00	1	3	1.26	-0.01	2.01
31	25	1.32	0	20	4.07	-0.28	2.92
32	11	1.27	1	6	1.79	0.21	2.33
33	64	2.52	1	50	6.55	0.91	4.12
34	11	7.82	1	75	22.30	-5.36	21.00
36	1	0.00	0	0	-	-	-

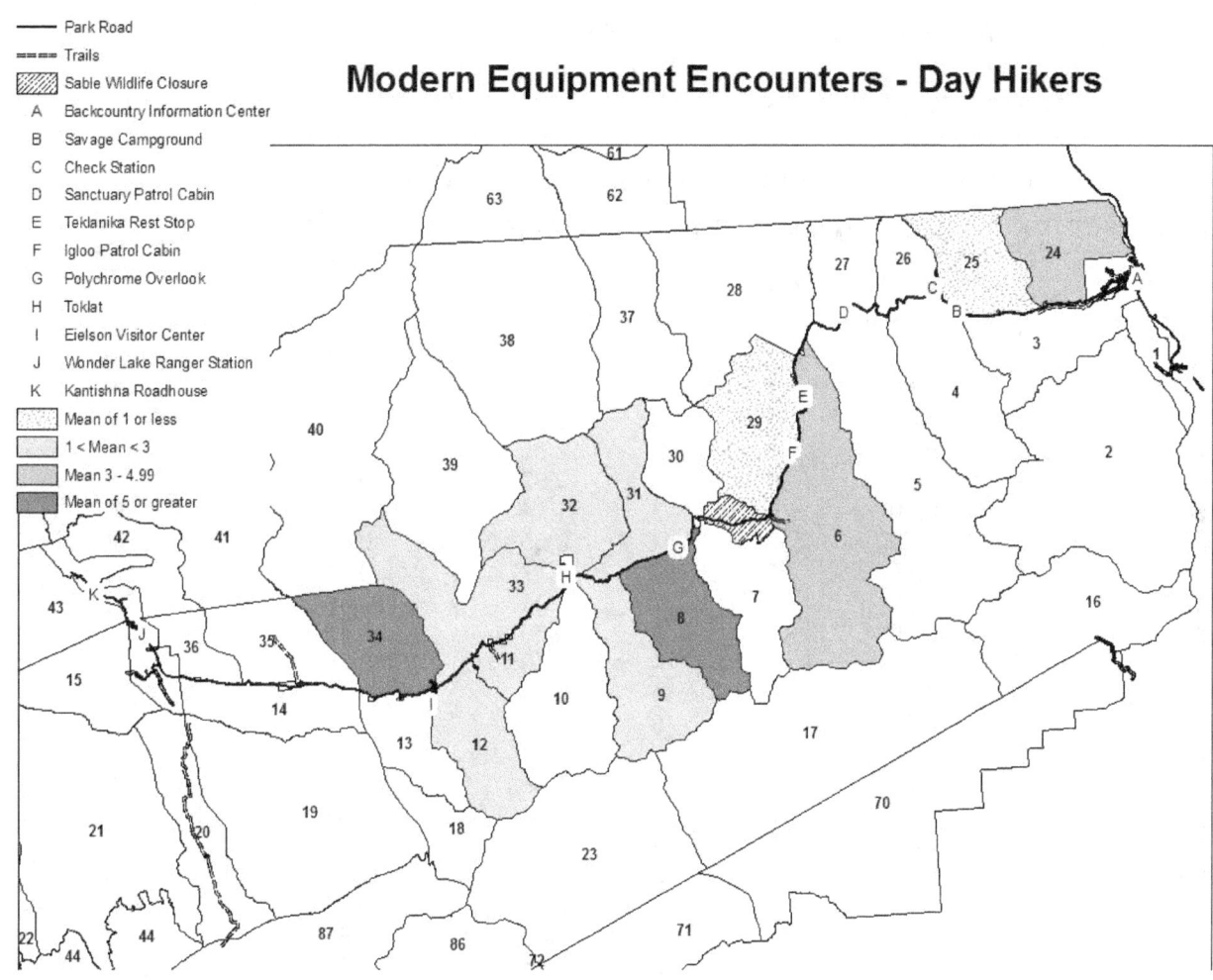

Figure 11. Distribution of Mean Level of Modern Equipment as Reported by Day Hikers, for Units with n > = 10.

Landscape Modifications: standard = none visible.

- Examining units with n > = 10 (n = 12), reveals 12 units with 95% confidence intervals (CI) of the means above zero.

Table 53. Mean Level of Landscape Modifications Reported by Day Hikers, by Unit.

Unit	n	Mean	Median	Max	SD	95% CI lower	95% CI upper
1	6	1.17	1	2	0.75	0.56	1.77
2	1	2.00	2	2	-	-	-
3	1	3.00	3	3	-	-	-
4	5	1.60	1	4	1.82	0.01	3.19
5	2	0.50	1	1	0.71	-0.48	1.48
6	19	1.47	1	5	1.39	0.85	2.10
7	3	2.00	1	5	2.65	-0.99	4.99
8	11	0.64	0	3	0.92	0.09	1.18
9	10	0.80	0	3	1.14	0.10	1.50
10	5	0.40	0	1	0.55	-0.08	0.88
11	27	0.85	1	5	1.17	0.41	1.29
12	50	1.30	1	20	2.94	0.48	2.12
13	5	0.60	1	1	0.55	0.12	1.08
14	7	1.57	1	4	1.40	0.54	2.61
15	3	0.33	0	1	0.58	-0.32	0.99
20	1	0.00	0	0	-	-	-
24	23	4.09	3	30	5.97	1.65	6.53
25	41	4.56	2	60	9.85	1.54	7.58
26	8	1.25	1	3	1.04	0.53	1.97
27	1	2.00	2	2	-	-	-
28	5	2.80	3	5	1.92	1.11	4.49
29	24	1.21	0	10	2.17	0.34	2.08
30	6	1.83	2	4	1.47	0.66	3.01
31	24	1.54	1	5	1.64	0.89	2.20
32	11	1.36	1	3	1.12	0.70	2.03
33	63	1.67	1	10	2.03	1.16	2.17
34	11	3.91	1	30	8.75	-1.26	9.08
36	1	1.00	1	1	-	-	-

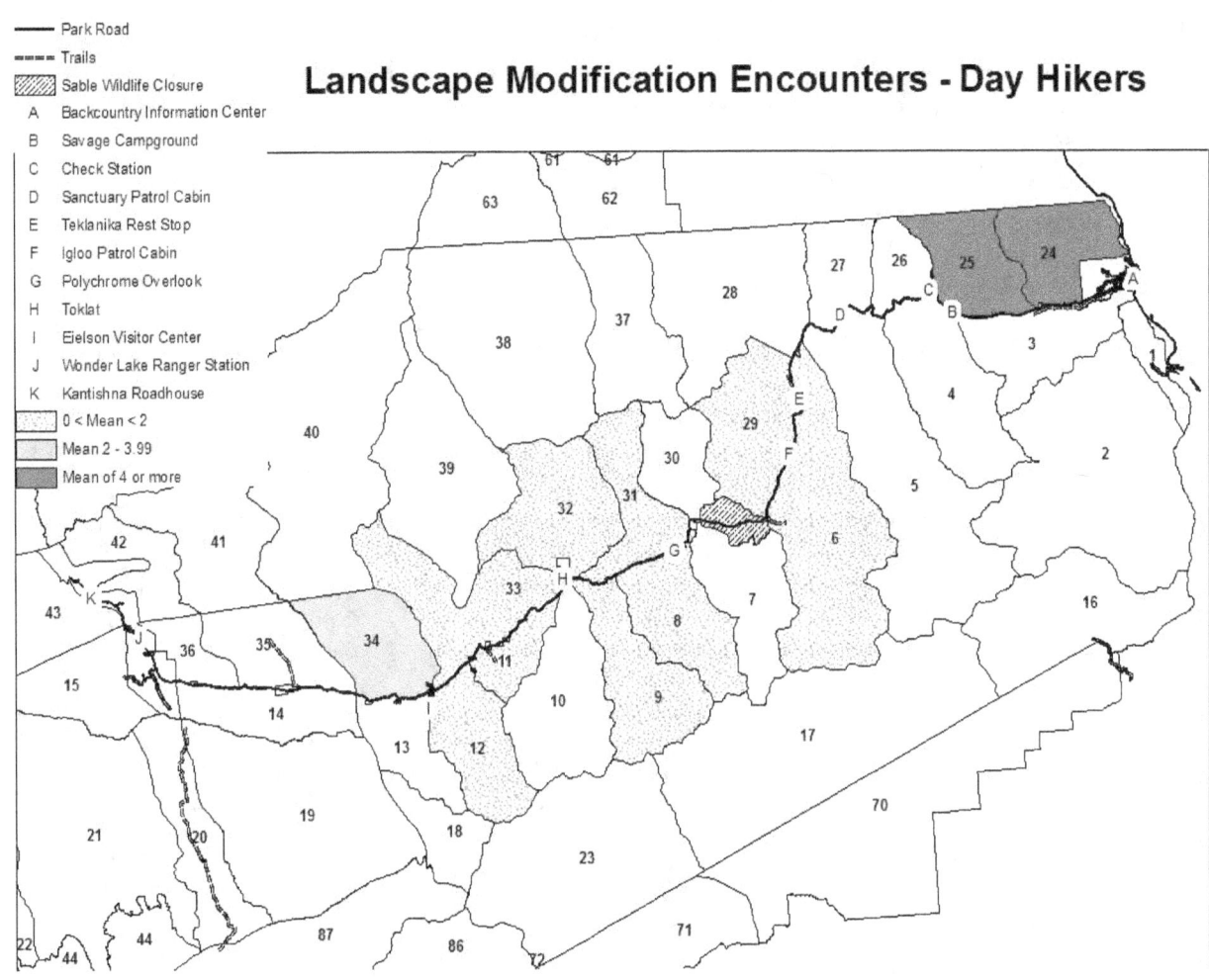

Figure 12. Distribution of Mean Level of Landscape Modifications as Reported by Day Hikers, for Units with n > = 10.

Other Park Visitors: standard = no more than two.
- Examining units with n > = 10 (n = 12), reveals five units with 95% confidence intervals (CI) of the mean above two.
- However, for the three units with n > = 10 and 95% CIs that overlap two, statistical power is low, and, thus, there is a high probability of incorrectly concluding the standard is not violated.

Table 54. Mean Level of Encounters with Other Park Visitors Reported by Day Hikers, by Unit.

Unit	n	Mean	Median	Max	SD	95% CI lower	95% CI upper
1	6	2.33	2	8	3.01	-0.08	4.74
2	1	15.00	15	15	-	-	-
3	1	8.00	8	8	-	-	-
4	6	5.33	4	20	7.37	-0.56	11.23
5	2	1.00	1	2	1.41	-0.96	2.96
6	20	0.90	1	3	1.07	0.43	1.37
7	3	2.00	2	4	2.00	-0.26	4.26
8	10	0.80	1	2	0.79	0.31	1.29
9	10	1.50	1	5	1.65	0.48	2.52
10	5	1.80	0	5	2.49	-0.38	3.98
11	31	1.19	1	4	1.19	0.77	1.61
12	51	7.59	3	50	11.71	4.37	10.80
13	5	1.60	1	3	1.34	0.42	2.78
14	7	2.86	2	12	4.10	-0.18	5.89
15	3	8.00	10	11	4.36	3.07	12.93
20	1	3.00	3	3	-	-	-
24	27	9.59	10	30	6.99	6.96	12.23
25	43	17.05	10	100	21.93	10.49	23.60
26	8	8.13	5	40	13.38	-1.15	17.40
27	1	0.00	0	0	-	-	-
28	4	2.75	1	10	4.86	-2.01	7.51
29	25	1.56	1	20	3.93	0.02	3.10
30	6	0.67	1	2	0.82	0.01	1.32
31	24	1.25	1	4	1.19	0.77	1.73
32	10	1.60	1	5	1.71	0.54	2.66
33	64	7.08	5	30	7.70	5.19	8.96
34	11	6.09	5	20	5.74	2.70	9.48
36	1	3.00	3	3	-	-	-

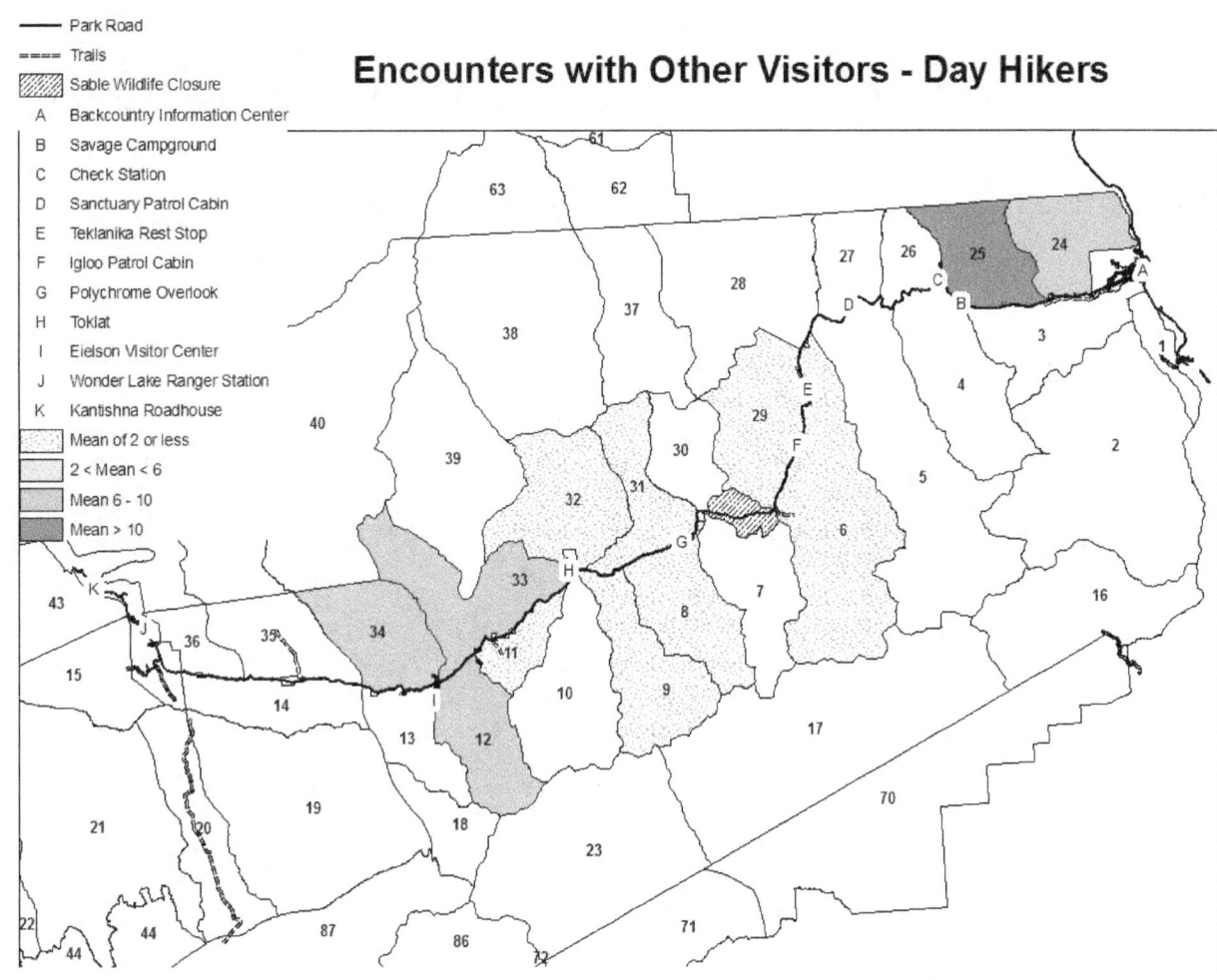

Figure 13. Distribution of Mean Level of Encounters with Other Visitors as Reported by Day Hikers, for Units with n > = 10.

Large Groups: standard = no more than two.

- Examining units with n > = 10 (n = 12), reveals no units with 95% confidence intervals (CI) of the mean above two and one unit with a 95% confidence interval that overlaps two.

Table 55. Mean Level of Encounters with Groups > 6 Reported by Day Hikers, by Unit.

Unit	n	Mean	Median	Max	SD	95% CI lower	95% CI upper
1	6	0.17	0	1	0.41	-0.16	0.49
2	1	1.00	1	1	-	-	-
3	1	0.00	0	0	-	-	-
4	6	0.17	0	1	0.41	-0.16	0.49
5	2	0.00	0	0	0.00	0.00	0.00
6	22	0.05	0	1	0.21	-0.04	0.13
7	3	0.67	0	2	1.15	-0.64	1.97
8	11	0.00	0	0	0.00	0.00	0.00
9	10	0.00	0	0	0.00	0.00	0.00
10	6	0.00	0	0	0.00	0.00	0.00
11	33	0.06	0	1	0.24	-0.02	0.14
12	56	1.07	0	10	2.03	0.54	1.60
13	4	0.75	0	3	1.50	-0.72	2.22
14	7	0.29	0	1	0.49	-0.08	0.65
15	3	1.33	1	3	1.53	-0.40	3.06
20	1	0.00	0	0	-	-	-
24	32	1.06	1	7	1.48	0.55	1.58
25	43	0.67	0	6	1.17	0.32	1.02
26	8	0.50	0	2	0.76	-0.02	1.02
27	1	0.00	0	0	-	-	-
28	5	2.40	0	10	4.34	-1.40	6.20
29	27	0.04	0	1	0.19	-0.04	0.11
30	7	0.00	0	0	0.00	0.00	0.00
31	23	0.22	0	1	0.42	0.05	0.39
32	12	0.08	0	1	0.29	-0.08	0.25
33	78	1.50	0	25	3.54	0.71	2.29
34	14	0.64	0	3	1.01	0.11	1.17
36	1	0.00	0	0	-	-	-

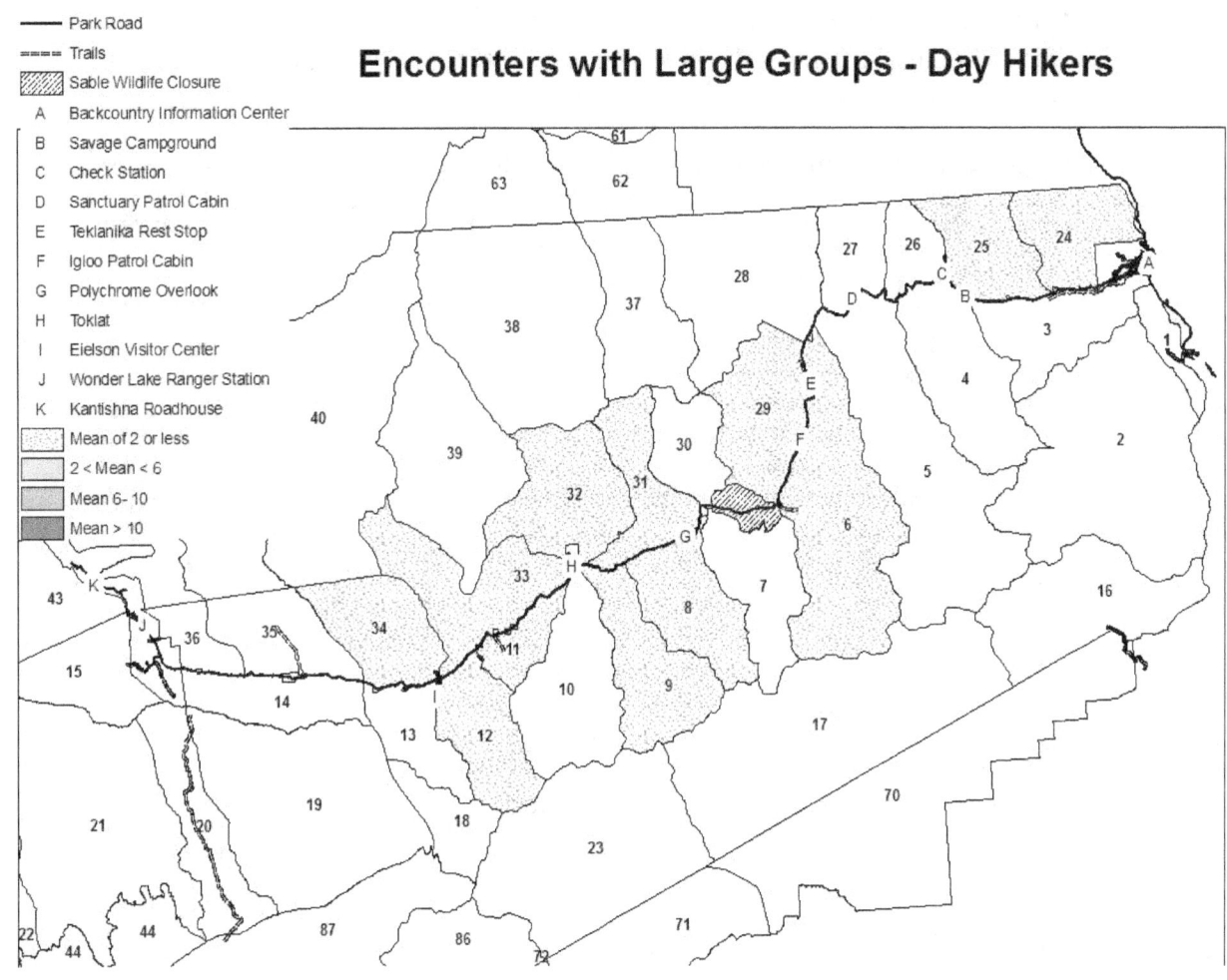

Figure 14. Distribution of Mean Level of Encounters with Groups > 6 as Reported by Day Hikers, for Units with n > = 10.

Encounters with NPS Rangers or Researchers: Standard = "routine."
- Examining units with n > = 10 (n = 13), reveals the level of contacts are low and the indicator is not being violated.

Table 56. Mean Level of Encounters with Rangers or Researchers Reported by Day Hikers, by Unit.

Unit	n	Mean	Median	Max	SD	95% CI lower	95% CI upper
1	6	0.17	0.0	1	0.41	-0.16	0.49
2	1	0.00	0.0	0	-	-	-
3	1	0.00	0.0	0	-	-	-
4	6	0.50	0.0	2	0.84	-0.17	1.17
5	2	0.00	0.0	0	-	-	-
6	22	0.18	0.0	2	0.50	-0.03	0.39
7	3	0.00	0.0	0	-	-	-
8	11	0.36	0.0	1	0.50	0.07	0.66
9	10	0.30	0.0	1	0.48	0.00	0.60
10	6	0.50	0.5	1	0.55	0.06	0.94
11	33	0.48	0.0	4	0.87	0.19	0.78
12	56	0.71	0.0	3	0.99	0.46	0.97
13	5	0.40	0.0	1	0.55	-0.08	0.88
14	7	0.14	0.0	1	0.38	-0.14	0.42
15	3	0.00	0.0	0	-	-	-
20	1	0.00	0.0	0	-	-	-
24	33	0.18	0.0	2	0.46	0.02	0.34
25	44	0.89	1.0	5	1.04	0.58	1.19
26	8	0.88	0.5	3	1.13	0.09	1.66
27	1	0.00	0.0	0	-	-	-
28	5	0.60	1.0	1	0.55	0.12	1.08
29	26	0.31	0.0	1	0.47	0.13	0.49
30	7	0.29	0.0	1	0.49	-0.08	0.65
31	24	0.29	0.0	2	0.62	0.04	0.54
32	12	0.42	0.0	3	0.90	-0.09	0.93
33	81	1.19	1.0	15	2.01	0.75	1.62
34	14	0.64	1.0	2	0.63	0.31	0.97
36	1	1.00	1.0	1	-	-	-

Litter or Human Waste: standard = less than 5% seeing.

- Examining units with n > = 10 (n = 13), reveals 1 units with 95% confidence intervals (CI) of the proportion above 5%.
- However, for the 12 units with n > = 10 and 95% CIs that overlap 5%, statistical power is low, and, thus, there is a high probability of incorrectly concluding the standard is not violated.

Table 57. Percent of Day Hikers Encountering Litter or Human Waste, by Unit.

Unit	n	Saw litter or human waste	Estimated population[1]	95% CI lower	95% CI upper
1	6	0.0%	-	0.0%	0.0%
2	1	0.0%	30	0.0%	0.0%
3	1	0.0%	-	0.0%	0.0%
4	6	33.3%	-	-3.9%	70.5%
5	2	0.0%	60	0.0%	0.0%
6	22	4.5%	662	-4.0%	13.1%
7	3	0.0%	90	0.0%	0.0%
8	11	18.2%	331	-4.3%	40.6%
9	10	30.0%	301	2.0%	58.0%
10	6	16.7%	181	-12.7%	46.1%
11	33	6.1%	993	-1.9%	14.1%
12	56	12.5%	1685	4.0%	21.0%
13	5	20.0%	150	-14.6%	54.6%
14	7	57.1%	211	21.0%	93.3%
15	3	0.0%	90	0.0%	0.0%
20	1	100.0%	30	100.0%	100.0%
24	33	33.3%	-	17.3%	49.4%
25	45	8.9%	-	0.6%	17.2%
26	8	12.5%	241	-10.1%	35.1%
27	1	0.0%	30	0.0%	0.0%
28	5	40.0%	150	-2.4%	82.4%
29	26	19.2%	782	4.3%	34.1%
30	7	14.3%	211	-11.3%	39.8%
31	25	16.0%	752	1.9%	30.1%
32	12	8.3%	361	-7.1%	23.7%
33	82	8.5%	2468	2.6%	14.5%
34	14	14.3%	421	-3.8%	32.3%
36	1	0.0%	30	0.0%	0.0%

[1]The confidence interval needs to account for the total population so an estimate of total population (i.e., "estimated population") was calculated as follows.

- Assumes 5% of passengers on buses hike. Using the estimate of 260,000 passengers on buses results in 13,000 total day hikers. For each unit, the percent it was represented in the sample was multiplied by 13,000 to estimate the population of that unit.
- This method was not applied to units 1, 2, 4, 24 and 25 as those units can be accessed by private vehicles.

Factors Affecting Mean Level of Indicators for Day Hikers: The influence of distance from park road, length of hike, weather and month of hike on the level of the indicators was examined.

Distance from Road: Day hikers were asked if they hiked farther than ½ mile from the park road. For those who did hike farther than ½ mile from the park road, they were to report the level of indicators they encountered only farther than ½ mile from the road. It does not appear that being farther than ½ mile from the road influenced the level of the indicators. The only exception is encounters with NPS personnel, with a higher level reported within ½ mile of the road (Table 58).

Table 58. Influence of Hiking Farther than Half a Mile from the Park Road on Indicators, Day Hikers.

	Hiked more than ½ mile from road	Did not hike more than ½ mile from road	t	p
Motorized sound encounters				
Mean	3.3	2.4	0.71	0.475
n	359	25		
Std. Dev.	5.9	3.2		
Modern equipment encounters				
Mean	2.1	1.8	0.18	0.854
n	361	26		
Std. Dev.	6.7	2.1		
Landscape modifications				
Mean	2.0	1.7	0.27	0.789
n	353	26		
Std. Dev.	4.5	1.7		
Encounters w/other park visitors				
Mean	5.7	8.0	-1.10	0.273
n	363	28		
Std. Dev.	10.4	14.2		
Encounters w/groups of size >6				
Mean	.6	1.5	-1.11	0.278
n	398	30		
Std. Dev.	1.5	4.6		
Encounters with NPS personnel				
Mean	.6	1.1	-2.27	0.024
n	406	28		
Std. Dev.	1.2	1.0		

Weather: Weather did not appear to influence the level indicators (Table 59).

Table 59. Influence of Weather on Indicators, Day Hikers.

	Sunny / Mostly sunny[1]	Cloudy	Rainy	F / Welch	Sig.
Motorized sound encounters					
Mean	3.4	3.4	2.3	1.27	0.282
n	206	98	84		
Std. Dev.	6.0	6.6	3.6		
Modern equipment encounters					
Mean	2.1	2.6	1.2	1.08	0.341
n	209	97	84		
Std. Dev.	6.2	8.7	3.1		
Landscape modifications					
Mean	1.8	2.6	1.4	2.26^2	0.107
n	200	98	84		
Std. Dev.	4.5	5.3	1.8		
Encounters w/other park visitors					
Mean	5.0	7.8	5.9	1.55^2	0.215
n	207	99	88		
Std. Dev.	7.8	15.5	9.4		
Encounters w/groups of size >6					
Mean	0.7	0.8	0.5	0.40	0.674
n	231	108	93		
Std. Dev.	2.3	1.4	1.4		
Encounters with NPS personnel					
Mean	0.6	0.7	0.6	0.14	0.867
n	235	111	92		
Std. Dev.	1.3	1.0	0.8		

[1]Weather was recorded at the Wilderness Access Center.
[2]Unequal variance, the Welch statistic is presented.

Length of Hike: The reported length of hikes was placed into categories and the mean level of the indicators compared. Those on shorter hikes encountered a higher number of other visitors, which might be due to self-selection of units by visitors. No pattern emerged for encounters with groups larger than 6 or encounters with NPS personnel (Table 60).

Table 60. Impact of Length of Hike on Indicators, Day Hikers.

	<=1 hour	1 - 2[1]	2 - 3	3 - 4	4 - 5	5 - 6	>6	F / Welch	Sig.
Motorized sound encounters									
Mean	3.7	3.0	3.0	2.4	2.8	2.8	7.2	1.119^{2}	0.356
n	61	111	67	56	45	25	19		
Std. Dev.	8.4	4.9	6.7	2.8	3.2	2.7	8.6		
Modern equipment encounters									
Mean	1.9	1.7	2.7	1.3	1.8	1.3	6.7	$.868^{2}$	0.521
n	63	114	67	56	44	24	18		
Std. Dev.	5.3	5.0	9.8	2.4	6.1	2.2	12.3		
Landscape modifications									
Mean	2.3	2.8	1.9	1.4	0.9	1.2	1.2	1.599	0.146
n	61	109	68	55	41	25	19		
Std. Dev.	4.1	6.5	3.8	1.8	1.1	2.1	1.6		
Encounters w/other park visitors									
Mean[3]	10.4^{a}	7.3^{a}	6.6^{ac}	3.3^{ab}	2.2^{b}	2.3^{bc}	2.1^{b}	6.987^{2}	< 0.001
n	62	111	71	57	46	24	19		
Std. Dev.	17.3	11.3	9.1	6.0	3.6	4.5	2.8		
Encounters w/groups of size >6									
Mean	1.2^{ab}	0.8^{a}	0.5^{ab}	0.7^{ab}	0.3^{ab}	0.2^{b}	0.2^{ab}	3.133^{2}	0.007
n	70	125	78	62	49	25	19		
Std. Dev.	3.3	1.8	0.9	2.0	1.1	0.4	0.7		
Encounters with NPS personnel									
Mean	0.8^{abc}	0.7^{a}	0.6^{ab}	0.5^{ab}	0.4^{bc}	0.3^{abc}	0.1^{c}	6.934^{2}	< 0.001
n	69	129	80	62	49	25	20		
Std. Dev.	2.0	1.0	1.2	0.7	0.6	0.6	0.3		

[1]Hours = Lower values 1 = 1.01, 2 = 2.01, 3 = 3.01, 4 = 4.01, 5 = 5.01.
[2]Unequal variance, the Welch statistic is presented.
[3]Means with different superscripts were significantly different at p = .05.

Month of Hike: The month in which the hike took place was not related to the level of the indicators (Table 61).

Table 61. Impact of Month on Indicators, Day Hikers.

	Month			F / Welch	Sig.
	June	July	August		
Motorized sound encounters					
Mean	3.17	2.91	3.64	0.56	0.573
n	96	184	108		
Std. Dev.	4.67	5.06	7.38		
Modern equipment encounters					
Mean	2.97	1.53	2.01	1.08[1]	0.343
n	95	183	112		
Std. Dev.	10.23	3.88	5.50		
Landscape modifications					
Mean	1.74	1.77	2.38	0.83	0.437
n	93	176	113		
Std. Dev.	3.32	3.17	6.19		
Encounters w/other park visitors					
Mean	5.04	5.65	6.96	0.94	0.391
n	98	182	114		
Std. Dev.	6.62	9.64	14.31		
Encounters w/groups of size >6					
Mean	.68	.81	.47	1.23	0.294
n	109	195	128		
Std. Dev.	2.66	1.83	1.13		
Encounters with NPS personnel					
Mean	0.69	0.62	0.51	0.76	0.468
n	110	195	133		
Std. Dev.	1.56	0.96	0.98		
Seeing Litter and Human Waste[2]					
% seeing	11.9%	14.6%	14.9%	0.55	0.760
n	109	198	114		

[1]Unequal variance, the Welch statistic is presented.
[2]Seeing litter or human waste was measured with a dichotomous variable and a test of the means is not appropriate. A chi-square test of association was conducted and the results presented in the table.

Level of Indicators Reported as Zero Tolerance: This section evaluates the standards from an absolute perspective; if one person reports a level above the standard, the standard is violated. For this analysis, when examining results by unit, small sample sizes are not an issue when the standard is violated. However, caution should be used in generalizing results from units with small *n*s in which the standard was not violated.

Percent of Respondents for Which the Standards are Violated: The distribution of data for the levels of the indicators was collapsed into a category of not exceeding the standard and several categories above the standard. Data were analyzed by the 28 units in which day hikers hiked. Results show that except for encounters with large groups, there were few units that were not violating the standard.

- Motorized sound: only one unit did *not* have at least one person for which the standard was exceeded (Table 62).
- Encounters with modern equipment: only four units did *not* have at least one person for which the standard was exceeded (Table 63).
- Encounters with landscape modification: only one unit did *not* have at least one person for which the standard was exceeded (Table 64).
- Encounters with other park visitors: only four units did *not* have at least one person for which the standard was exceeded (Table 65).
- Encounters with groups larger than six: eight units had at least one person for which the standard was exceeded (Table 66).
- Litter or human Waste: 20 units had at least one person for which the standard was exceeded (data displayed in Table 57 of previous section).

Table 62. Motorized Sound Distribution, Day hikers.

Unit	n	< = 1	2 – 5	6 – 10	> 10	Percent above standard
1	6	66.7%	16.7%	0.0%	16.7%	33.4%
2	1	0.0%	100.0%	0.0%	0.0%	100.0%
3	1	0.0%	100.0%	0.0%	0.0%	100.0%
4	5	60.0%	40.0%	0.0%	0.0%	40.0%
5	2	50.0%	50.0%	0.0%	0.0%	50.0%
6	17	35.3%	35.3%	5.9%	23.5%	64.7%
7	3	33.3%	66.7%	0.0%	0.0%	66.7%
8	11	36.4%	54.5%	0.0%	0.0%	54.5%
9	9	22.2%	66.7%	11.1%	0.0%	77.8%
10	5	40.0%	40.0%	20.0%	0.0%	60.0%
11	31	48.4%	29.0%	16.1%	6.5%	51.6%
12	46	60.9%	26.1%	8.7%	4.3%	39.1%
13	5	80.0%	0.0%	0.0%	20.0%	20.0%
14	7	57.1%	28.6%	14.3%	0.0%	42.9%
15	3	0.0%	100.0%	0.0%	0.0%	100.0%
20	1	100.0%	0.0%	0.0%	0.0%	0.0%
24	29	34.5%	48.3%	6.9%	10.3%	65.5%
25	40	62.5%	32.5%	5.0%	0.0%	37.5%
26	7	28.6%	71.4%	0.0%	0.0%	71.4%
27	1	0.0%	100.0%	0.0%	0.0%	100.0%
28	5	60.0%	20.0%	20.0%	0.0%	40.0%
29	23	52.2%	43.5%	4.3%	0.0%	47.8%
30	6	66.7%	33.3%	0.0%	0.0%	33.3%
31	24	41.7%	37.5%	12.5%	8.3%	58.3%
32	11	54.5%	27.3%	9.1%	9.1%	45.5%
33	67	46.3%	38.8%	14.9%	0.0%	53.7%
34	13	46.2%	38.5%	15.4%	0.0%	53.9%
36	1	0.0%	100.0%	0.0%	0.0%	100.0%

Table 63. Modern Equipment Distribution, Day hikers.

Unit	n	< = 1	2 – 5	6 – 10	> 10	Percent above standard
1	6	66.7%	33.3%	0.0%	0.0%	33.3%
2	1	0.0%	100.0%	0.0%	0.0%	100.0%
3	1	0.0%	100.0%	0.0%	0.0%	100.0%
4	5	80.0%	20.0%	0.0%	0.0%	20.0%
5	2	100.0%	0.0%	0.0%	0.0%	0.0%
6	17	64.7%	17.6%	11.8%	5.9%	35.3%
7	3	100.0%	0.0%	0.0%	0.0%	0.0%
8	11	54.5%	27.3%	9.1%	9.1%	45.5%
9	10	70.0%	30.0%	0.0%	0.0%	30.0%
10	5	100.0%	0.0%	0.0%	0.0%	0.0%
11	31	77.4%	12.9%	3.2%	6.5%	22.6%
12	52	78.8%	17.3%	1.9%	1.9%	21.1%
13	5	40.0%	20.0%	40.0%	0.0%	60.0%
14	7	71.4%	28.6%	0.0%	0.0%	28.6%
15	3	66.7%	33.3%	0.0%	0.0%	33.3%
20	1	0.0%	100.0%	0.0%	0.0%	100.0%
24	27	66.7%	22.2%	3.7%	7.4%	33.3%
25	42	83.3%	16.7%	0.0%	0.0%	16.7%
26	7	71.4%	28.6%	0.0%	0.0%	28.6%
27	1	0.0%	100.0%	0.0%	0.0%	100.0%
28	5	80.0%	20.0%	0.0%	0.0%	20.0%
29	23	78.3%	21.7%	0.0%	0.0%	21.7%
30	6	66.7%	33.3%	0.0%	0.0%	33.3%
31	25	84.0%	12.0%	0.0%	4.0%	16.0%
32	11	81.8%	9.1%	9.1%	0.0%	18.2%
33	64	65.6%	23.4%	9.4%	1.6%	34.4%
34	11	63.6%	27.3%	0.0%	9.1%	36.4%
36	1	100.0%	0.0%	0.0%	0.0%	0.0%

Table 64. Landscape Modification Distribution, Day Hikers.

Unit	n	0	1 – 5	6 – 10	> 10	Percent above standard
1	6	16.7%	83.3%	0.0%	0.0%	83.3%
2	1	0.0%	100.0%	0.0%	0.0%	100.0%
3	1	0.0%	100.0%	0.0%	0.0%	100.0%
4	5	40.0%	60.0%	0.0%	0.0%	60.0%
5	2	50.0%	50.0%	0.0%	0.0%	50.0%
6	19	26.3%	73.7%	0.0%	0.0%	73.7%
7	3	33.3%	66.7%	0.0%	0.0%	66.7%
8	11	54.5%	45.5%	0.0%	0.0%	45.5%
9	10	60.0%	40.0%	0.0%	0.0%	40.0%
10	5	60.0%	40.0%	0.0%	0.0%	40.0%
11	27	40.7%	59.3%	0.0%	0.0%	59.3%
12	50	46.0%	52.0%	0.0%	2.0%	54.0%
13	5	40.0%	60.0%	0.0%	0.0%	60.0%
14	7	14.3%	85.7%	0.0%	0.0%	85.7%
15	3	66.7%	33.3%	0.0%	0.0%	33.3%
20	1	100.0%	0.0%	0.0%	0.0%	0.0%
24	23	8.7%	78.3%	8.7%	4.3%	91.3%
25	41	7.3%	80.5%	4.9%	7.3%	92.7%
26	8	25.0%	75.0%	0.0%	0.0%	75.0%
27	1	0.0%	100.0%	0.0%	0.0%	100.0%
28	5	20.0%	80.0%	0.0%	0.0%	80.0%
29	24	54.2%	41.7%	4.2%	0.0%	45.8%
30	6	16.7%	83.3%	0.0%	0.0%	83.3%
31	24	37.5%	62.5%	0.0%	0.0%	62.5%
32	11	18.2%	81.8%	0.0%	0.0%	81.8%
33	63	27.0%	69.8%	3.2%	0.0%	73.0%
34	11	27.3%	63.6%	0.0%	9.1%	72.7%
36	1	0.0%	100.0%	0.0%	0.0%	100.0%

Table 65. Encounters with Other Park Visitors Distribution, Day Hikers.

Unit	n	0 - 2	3 – 5	6 – 10	> 10	Percent above standard
1	6	66.7%	16.7%	16.7%	0.0%	33.4%
2	1	0.0%	0.0%	0.0%	100.0%	100.0%
3	1	0.0%	0.0%	100.0%	0.0%	100.0%
4	6	33.3%	50.0%	0.0%	16.7%	66.7%
5	2	100.0%	0.0%	0.0%	0.0%	0.0%
6	20	85.0%	15.0%	0.0%	0.0%	15.0%
7	3	66.7%	33.3%	0.0%	0.0%	33.3%
8	10	100.0%	0.0%	0.0%	0.0%	0.0%
9	10	80.0%	20.0%	0.0%	0.0%	20.0%
10	5	60.0%	40.0%	0.0%	0.0%	40.0%
11	31	80.6%	19.4%	0.0%	0.0%	19.4%
12	51	41.2%	29.4%	11.8%	17.6%	58.8%
13	5	60.0%	40.0%	0.0%	0.0%	40.0%
14	7	85.7%	0.0%	0.0%	14.3%	14.3%
15	3	0.0%	33.3%	33.3%	33.3%	100.0%
20	1	0.0%	100.0%	0.0%	0.0%	100.0%
24	27	11.1%	25.9%	37.0%	25.9%	88.9%
25	43	9.3%	16.3%	32.6%	41.9%	90.7%
26	8	37.5%	12.5%	37.5%	12.5%	62.5%
27	1	100.0%	0.0%	0.0%	0.0%	0.0%
28	4	75.0%	0.0%	25.0%	0.0%	25.0%
29	25	92.0%	4.0%	0.0%	4.0%	8.0%
30	6	100.0%	0.0%	0.0%	0.0%	0.0%
31	24	83.3%	16.7%	0.0%	0.0%	16.7%
32	10	80.0%	20.0%	0.0%	0.0%	20.0%
33	64	35.9%	17.2%	26.6%	20.3%	64.1%
34	11	18.2%	36.4%	36.4%	9.1%	81.8%
36	1	0.0%	100.0%	0.0%	0.0%	100.0%

Table 66. Encounters with Groups >6 Distribution, Day Hikers.

Unit	n	0 - 2	3 – 5	6 – 10	> 10	Percent above standard
1	6	100.0%	0.0%	0.0%	0.0%	0.0%
2	1	100.0%	0.0%	0.0%	0.0%	0.0%
3	1	100.0%	0.0%	0.0%	0.0%	0.0%
4	6	100.0%	0.0%	0.0%	0.0%	0.0%
5	2	100.0%	0.0%	0.0%	0.0%	0.0%
6	22	100.0%	0.0%	0.0%	0.0%	0.0%
7	3	100.0%	0.0%	0.0%	0.0%	0.0%
8	11	100.0%	0.0%	0.0%	0.0%	0.0%
9	10	100.0%	0.0%	0.0%	0.0%	0.0%
10	6	100.0%	0.0%	0.0%	0.0%	0.0%
11	33	100.0%	0.0%	0.0%	0.0%	0.0%
12	56	87.5%	7.1%	5.4%	0.0%	12.5%
13	4	75.0%	25.0%	0.0%	0.0%	25.0%
14	7	100.0%	0.0%	0.0%	0.0%	0.0%
15	3	66.7%	33.3%	0.0%	0.0%	33.3%
20	1	100.0%	0.0%	0.0%	0.0%	0.0%
24	32	90.6%	6.3%	3.1%	0.0%	9.4%
25	43	95.3%	2.3%	2.3%	0.0%	4.6%
26	8	100.0%	0.0%	0.0%	0.0%	0.0%
27	1	100.0%	0.0%	0.0%	0.0%	0.0%
28	5	80.0%	0.0%	20.0%	0.0%	20.0%
29	27	100.0%	0.0%	0.0%	0.0%	0.0%
30	7	100.0%	0.0%	0.0%	0.0%	0.0%
31	23	100.0%	0.0%	0.0%	0.0%	0.0%
32	12	100.0%	0.0%	0.0%	0.0%	0.0%
33	78	85.9%	5.1%	6.4%	2.6%	14.1%
34	14	92.9%	7.1%	0.0%	0.0%	7.1%
36	1	100.0%	0.0%	0.0%	0.0%	0.0%

Percent of Days Standards are Violated: If a zero tolerance definition of when a standard is violated is adopted, the number of days in which a standard was violated can be calculated.

Day hikers hiked on 69 different days:
- The motorized sound standard was violated on 62 days (Table 67).
- The modern equipment standard was violated on 52 days (Table 68).
- The landscape modification standard was violated on 67 days (Table 69).
- The encounters with other park visitors standard was violated on 57 days (Table 70).
- The encounters with large groups standard was violated on 23 days (Table 71).
- The litter and human waste standard was violated on 35 days (Table 72), however, the low *n*s of some units skewed the percentage seeing litter or human waste.

Table 67. Percent of Day Hikers Reporting the Motorized Sound Standard was Violated, by Day.

Date	% > 1	n	Date	% > 1	n	Date	% > 1	n
1-Jun-10	100.0	2	1-Jul-10	62.5	8	1-Aug-10	60.0	5
2-Jun-10	75.0	4	2-Jul-10	33.3	6	2-Aug-10	50.0	4
3-Jun-10	33.3	3	4-Jul-10	50.0	6	3-Aug-10	100.0	1
5-Jun-10	100.0	1	5-Jul-10	50.0	4	7-Aug-10	100.0	1
6-Jun-10	0.0	2	6-Jul-10	20.0	10	8-Aug-10	60.0	5
7-Jun-10	100.0	5	7-Jul-10	55.6	9	9-Aug-10	25.0	4
8-Jun-10	0.0	5	10-Jul-10	16.7	6	10-Aug-10	71.4	7
9-Jun-10	66.7	3	11-Jul-10	50.0	6	11-Aug-10	60.0	5
10-Jun-10	100.0	1	13-Jul-10	50.0	8	12-Aug-10	30.0	10
12-Jun-10	50.0	2	14-Jul-10	0.0	6	13-Aug-10	50.0	2
13-Jun-10	100.0	2	16-Jul-10	100.0	1	14-Aug-10	57.1	7
15-Jun-10	25.0	4	18-Jul-10	58.3	12	15-Aug-10	50.0	8
16-Jun-10	20.0	5	20-Jul-10	45.5	11	16-Aug-10	37.5	8
17-Jun-10	0.0	3	22-Jul-10	82.4	17	17-Aug-10	66.7	3
18-Jun-10	60.0	5	25-Jul-10	50.0	12	18-Aug-10	50.0	4
19-Jun-10	100.0	5	26-Jul-10	60.0	10	19-Aug-10	100.0	1
21-Jun-10	66.7	6	27-Jul-10	33.3	6	20-Aug-10	66.7	3
23-Jun-10	62.5	8	28-Jul-10	40.0	20	21-Aug-10	40.0	5
24-Jun-10	25.0	4	29-Jul-10	60.0	10	22-Aug-10	33.3	3
25-Jun-10	100.0	1	31-Jul-10	62.5	16	23-Aug-10	72.7	11
27-Jun-10	33.3	12				24-Aug-10	0.0	1
28-Jun-10	57.1	7				25-Aug-10	71.4	7
29-Jun-10	33.3	3				26-Aug-10	100.0	2
30-Jun-10	66.7	3				27-Aug-10	0.0	1

Note: due to missing data there were only 68 days for which the level of motorized sounds was reported.

Table 68. Percent of Day Hikers Reporting the Modern Equipment Standard was Violated, by Day.

Date	% > 1	n	Date	% > 1	n	Date	% > 1	n
1-Jun-10	50.0	2	1-Jul-10	42.9	7	1-Aug-10	57.1	7
2-Jun-10	0.0	3	2-Jul-10	33.3	6	2-Aug-10	20.0	5
3-Jun-10	0.0	3	4-Jul-10	33.3	6	3-Aug-10	100.0	1
5-Jun-10	100.0	1	5-Jul-10	20.0	5	7-Aug-10	100.0	1
6-Jun-10	0.0	2	6-Jul-10	10.0	10	8-Aug-10	60.0	5
7-Jun-10	60.0	5	7-Jul-10	0.0	9	9-Aug-10	50.0	4
8-Jun-10	0.0	4	10-Jul-10	16.7	6	10-Aug-10	16.7	6
9-Jun-10	33.3	3	11-Jul-10	16.7	6	11-Aug-10	20.0	5
10-Jun-10	100.0	1	13-Jul-10	25.0	8	12-Aug-10	45.5	11
12-Jun-10	0.0	2	14-Jul-10	16.7	6	13-Aug-10	50.0	2
13-Jun-10	0.0	1	16-Jul-10	100.0	1	14-Aug-10	30.0	10
15-Jun-10	0.0	4	18-Jul-10	8.3	12	15-Aug-10	20.0	5
16-Jun-10	40.0	5	20-Jul-10	9.1	11	16-Aug-10	37.5	8
17-Jun-10	0.0	3	22-Jul-10	23.5	17	17-Aug-10	0.0	4
18-Jun-10	20.0	5	25-Jul-10	41.7	12	18-Aug-10	40.0	5
19-Jun-10	50.0	6	26-Jul-10	40.0	10	19-Aug-10	0.0	1
21-Jun-10	16.7	6	27-Jul-10	40.0	5	20-Aug-10	0.0	1
23-Jun-10	25.0	8	28-Jul-10	15.0	20	21-Aug-10	20.0	5
24-Jun-10	0.0	4	29-Jul-10	30.0	10	22-Aug-10	33.3	3
25-Jun-10	100.0	1	31-Jul-10	37.5	16	23-Aug-10	27.3	11
27-Jun-10	25.0	12				24-Aug-10	0.0	1
28-Jun-10	25.0	8				25-Aug-10	28.6	7
29-Jun-10	33.3	3				26-Aug-10	0.0	3
30-Jun-10	33.3	3				27-Aug-10	0.0	1

Note: Due to missing data there were only 68 days for which the level of modern equipment was reported.

Table 69. Percent of Day Hikers Reporting the Landscape Modification Standard was Violated, by Day.

Date	% > 0	n	Date	% > 0	n	Date	% > 0	n
1-Jun-10	50.0	2	1-Jul-10	42.9	7	1-Aug-10	85.7	7
2-Jun-10	66.7	3	2-Jul-10	66.7	3	2-Aug-10	60.0	5
3-Jun-10	50.0	2	4-Jul-10	50.0	6	3-Aug-10	100.0	1
5-Jun-10	0.0	1	5-Jul-10	80.0	5	7-Aug-10	100.0	1
6-Jun-10	100.0	1	6-Jul-10	50.0	10	8-Aug-10	60.0	5
7-Jun-10	100.0	5	7-Jul-10	77.8	9	9-Aug-10	25.0	4
8-Jun-10	80.0	5	10-Jul-10	50.0	6	10-Aug-10	83.3	6
9-Jun-10	33.3	3	11-Jul-10	66.7	6	11-Aug-10	60.0	5
10-Jun-10	100.0	1	13-Jul-10	87.5	8	12-Aug-10	72.7	11
12-Jun-10	100.0	2	14-Jul-10	50.0	6	13-Aug-10	100.0	2
13-Jun-10	50.0	2	16-Jul-10	100.0	1	14-Aug-10	87.5	8
15-Jun-10	75.0	4	18-Jul-10	50.0	12	15-Aug-10	60.0	5
16-Jun-10	100.0	5	20-Jul-10	50.0	10	16-Aug-10	87.5	8
17-Jun-10	50.0	2	22-Jul-10	53.3	15	17-Aug-10	25.0	4
18-Jun-10	60.0	5	25-Jul-10	83.3	12	18-Aug-10	83.3	6
19-Jun-10	83.3	6	26-Jul-10	100.0	10	19-Aug-10	100.0	1
21-Jun-10	20.0	5	27-Jul-10	60.0	5	20-Aug-10	0.0	1
22-Jun-10	100.0	1	28-Jul-10	47.4	19	21-Aug-10	60.0	5
23-Jun-10	87.5	8	29-Jul-10	60.0	10	22-Aug-10	100.0	3
24-Jun-10	66.7	3	31-Jul-10	75.0	16	23-Aug-10	100.0	10
25-Jun-10	100.0	1				24-Aug-10	100.0	2
27-Jun-10	91.7	12				25-Aug-10	87.5	8
28-Jun-10	37.5	8				26-Aug-10	66.7	3
29-Jun-10	100.0	3				27-Aug-10	50.0	2
30-Jun-10	66.7	3						

Table 70. Percent of Day Hikers Reporting the Encounters with Other Visitors Standard was Violated, by Day.

Date	% > 2	n	Date	% > 2	n	Date	% > 2	n
1-Jun-10	0.0	2	1-Jul-10	44.4	9	1-Aug-10	50.0	6
2-Jun-10	0.0	3	2-Jul-10	33.3	6	2-Aug-10	60.0	5
3-Jun-10	33.3	3	4-Jul-10	16.7	6	3-Aug-10	0.0	1
5-Jun-10	0.0	1	5-Jul-10	75.0	4	7-Aug-10	0.0	1
6-Jun-10	100.0	1	6-Jul-10	60.0	10	8-Aug-10	40.0	5
7-Jun-10	40.0	5	7-Jul-10	57.1	7	9-Aug-10	0.0	4
8-Jun-10	20.0	5	10-Jul-10	50.0	6	10-Aug-10	83.3	6
9-Jun-10	66.7	3	11-Jul-10	16.7	6	11-Aug-10	40.0	5
10-Jun-10	100.0	1	13-Jul-10	22.2	9	12-Aug-10	54.5	11
12-Jun-10	50.0	2	14-Jul-10	0.0	6	13-Aug-10	0.0	2
13-Jun-10	50.0	2	16-Jul-10	0.0	1	14-Aug-10	77.8	9
15-Jun-10	50.0	4	18-Jul-10	58.3	12	15-Aug-10	60.0	5
16-Jun-10	100.0	5	20-Jul-10	27.3	11	16-Aug-10	57.1	7
17-Jun-10	50.0	2	22-Jul-10	43.8	16	17-Aug-10	25.0	4
18-Jun-10	40.0	5	25-Jul-10	66.7	12	18-Aug-10	40.0	5
19-Jun-10	50.0	6	26-Jul-10	80.0	10	19-Aug-10	0.0	1
21-Jun-10	0.0	6	27-Jul-10	40.0	5	20-Aug-10	50.0	2
22-Jun-10	100.0	1	28-Jul-10	42.1	19	21-Aug-10	60.0	5
23-Jun-10	11.1	9	29-Jul-10	36.4	11	22-Aug-10	33.3	3
24-Jun-10	0.0	3	31-Jul-10	50.0	16	23-Aug-10	100.0	12
25-Jun-10	100.0	1				24-Aug-10	50.0	2
27-Jun-10	84.6	13				25-Aug-10	62.5	8
28-Jun-10	55.6	9				26-Aug-10	33.3	3
29-Jun-10	66.7	3				27-Aug-10	50.0	2
30-Jun-10	66.7	3						

Table 71. Percent of Day Hikers Reporting the Encounters with Large Groups Standard was Violated, by Day.

Date	% > 2	n	Date	% > 2	n	Date	% > 2	n
1-Jun-10	0.0	3	1-Jul-10	10.0	10	1-Aug-10	0.0	7
2-Jun-10	0.0	5	2-Jul-10	0.0	7	2-Aug-10	0.0	5
3-Jun-10	0.0	4	4-Jul-10	14.3	7	3-Aug-10	0.0	1
5-Jun-10	0.0	1	5-Jul-10	33.3	6	7-Aug-10	0.0	1
6-Jun-10	0.0	2	6-Jul-10	11.1	9	8-Aug-10	20.0	5
7-Jun-10	20.0	5	7-Jul-10	11.1	9	9-Aug-10	0.0	4
8-Jun-10	0.0	5	10-Jul-10	0.0	6	10-Aug-10	28.6	7
9-Jun-10	0.0	4	11-Jul-10	0.0	6	11-Aug-10	0.0	4
10-Jun-10	0.0	1	13-Jul-10	0.0	9	12-Aug-10	0.0	11
12-Jun-10	0.0	2	14-Jul-10	0.0	6	13-Aug-10	0.0	2
13-Jun-10	0.0	4	16-Jul-10	0.0	1	14-Aug-10	10.0	10
15-Jun-10	0.0	4	18-Jul-10	7.7	13	15-Aug-10	12.5	8
16-Jun-10	0.0	5	20-Jul-10	8.3	12	16-Aug-10	0.0	9
17-Jun-10	0.0	3	22-Jul-10	0.0	19	17-Aug-10	16.7	6
18-Jun-10	0.0	6	25-Jul-10	8.3	12	18-Aug-10	0.0	7
19-Jun-10	16.7	6	26-Jul-10	22.2	9	19-Aug-10	0.0	1
21-Jun-10	0.0	6	27-Jul-10	16.7	6	20-Aug-10	0.0	4
22-Jun-10	0.0	1	28-Jul-10	9.5	21	21-Aug-10	0.0	6
23-Jun-10	0.0	9	29-Jul-10	9.1	11	22-Aug-10	33.3	3
24-Jun-10	0.0	4	31-Jul-10	6.3	16	23-Aug-10	0.0	12
27-Jun-10	7.1	14				24-Aug-10	0.0	2
28-Jun-10	11.1	9				25-Aug-10	0.0	8
29-Jun-10	0.0	3				26-Aug-10	0.0	3
30-Jun-10	0.0	3				27-Aug-10	0.0	2

Table 72. Percent of Day Hikers Seeing Litter and Human Waste, by Day.

Date	% seeing	n	Date	% seeing	n	Date	% seeing	n
01-Jun-2010	0%	3	01-Jul-2010	20%	10	01-Aug-2010	0%	9
02-Jun-2010	0%	5	02-Jul-2010	29%	7	02-Aug-2010	20%	5
03-Jun-2010	25%	4	04-Jul-2010	14%	7	03-Aug-2010	0%	1
05-Jun-2010	0%	1	05-Jul-2010	33%	6	07-Aug-2010	0%	1
06-Jun-2010	0%	2	06-Jul-2010	10%	10	08-Aug-2010	40%	5
07-Jun-2010	20%	5	07-Jul-2010	22%	9	09-Aug-2010	0%	4
08-Jun-2010	0%	5	10-Jul-2010	33%	6	10-Aug-2010	14%	7
09-Jun-2010	0%	3	11-Jul-2010	33%	6	11-Aug-2010	20%	5
10-Jun-2010	0%	1	13-Jul-2010	0%	9	12-Aug-2010	17%	12
12-Jun-2010	0%	2	14-Jul-2010	0%	6	13-Aug-2010	0%	2
13-Jun-2010	0%	4	16-Jul-2010	0%	1	14-Aug-2010	30%	10
15-Jun-2010	0%	4	18-Jul-2010	8%	13	15-Aug-2010	11%	9
16-Jun-2010	20%	5	20-Jul-2010	0%	12	16-Aug-2010	11%	9
17-Jun-2010	0%	3	22-Jul-2010	16%	19	17-Aug-2010	0%	6
18-Jun-2010	0%	6	25-Jul-2010	25%	12	18-Aug-2010	57%	7
19-Jun-2010	14%	7	26-Jul-2010	0%	10	19-Aug-2010	0%	1
21-Jun-2010	17%	6	27-Jul-2010	0%	7	20-Aug-2010	0%	4
22-Jun-2010	0%	1	28-Jul-2010	19%	21	21-Aug-2010	0%	6
23-Jun-2010	22%	9	29-Jul-2010	27%	11	22-Aug-2010	33%	3
24-Jun-2010	25%	4	31-Jul-2010	6%	16	23-Aug-2010	8%	12
25-Jun-2010	0%	1				24-Aug-2010	0%	2
27-Jun-2010	21%	14				25-Aug-2010	22%	9
28-Jun-2010	22%	9				26-Aug-2010	0%	3
29-Jun-2010	0%	3				27-Aug-2010	0%	2
30-Jun-2010	0%	2						

Percent of Time Encountering Indicators: Respondents were asked what percent of time they encountered motorized sound, landscape modifications, modern equipment and other park visitors. Response categories were 0 – 24%, 25 – 49%, 50 – 74%, and 75 – 100%. In several units respondents encountered the standards 25% or more of the time (Table 73 – Table 76).

Table 73. Percent of Time Day Hikers Heard Motorized Sound per Day, by Unit.

Unit	n	0%[1]	1 – 24%	25 – 49%	50 – 74%	75 – 100%
1	6	33.3%	33.3%	0.0%	33.3%	0.0%
2	1	0.0%	0.0%	100.0%	0.0%	0.0%
3	1	0.0%	100.0%	0.0%	0.0%	0.0%
4	6	33.3%	50.0%	16.7%	0.0%	0.0%
5	2	50.0%	50.0%	0.0%	0.0%	0.0%
6	21	9.5%	81.0%	9.5%	0.0%	0.0%
7	3	0.0%	100.0%	0.0%	0.0%	0.0%
8	11	18.2%	54.5%	18.2%	9.1%	0.0%
9	10	20.0%	50.0%	30.0%	0.0%	0.0%
10	5	40.0%	60.0%	0.0%	0.0%	0.0%
11	33	33.3%	51.5%	9.1%	3.0%	3.0%
12	55	34.5%	47.3%	14.5%	3.6%	0.0%
13	5	40.0%	40.0%	20.0%	0.0%	0.0%
14	7	28.6%	57.1%	14.3%	0.0%	0.0%
15	3	0.0%	100.0%	0.0%	0.0%	0.0%
20	1	0.0%	100.0%	0.0%	0.0%	0.0%
24	33	18.2%	45.5%	12.1%	12.1%	12.1%
25	44	38.6%	50.0%	6.8%	4.5%	0.0%
26	8	25.0%	62.5%	12.5%	0.0%	0.0%
27	1	0.0%	100.0%	0.0%	0.0%	0.0%
28	5	40.0%	40.0%	20.0%	0.0%	0.0%
29	27	40.7%	48.1%	7.4%	0.0%	3.7%
30	7	28.6%	57.1%	14.3%	0.0%	0.0%
31	25	28.0%	56.0%	8.0%	8.0%	0.0%
32	12	8.3%	83.3%	0.0%	0.0%	8.3%
33	83	20.5%	63.9%	9.6%	4.8%	1.2%
34	14	35.7%	42.9%	21.4%	0.0%	0.0%
36	1	0.0%	100.0%	0.0%	0.0%	0.0%

[1]On the survey the lowest response category was 0 – 24%. The 0% category was created from those who reported they did not hear any motorized sounds.

Table 74. Percent of Time Day Hikers Saw Modern Equipment per Day, by Unit.

Unit	n	0%[1]	1 – 24%	25 – 49%	50 – 74%	75 – 100%
1	6	50.0%	33.3%	0.0%	16.7%	0.0%
2	1	0.0%	100.0%	0.0%	0.0%	0.0%
3	1	0.0%	100.0%	0.0%	0.0%	0.0%
4	6	50.0%	16.7%	16.7%	16.7%	0.0%
5	2	50.0%	0.0%	0.0%	50.0%	0.0%
6	22	45.5%	40.9%	4.5%	0.0%	9.1%
7	3	66.7%	33.3%	0.0%	0.0%	0.0%
8	11	45.5%	36.4%	9.1%	0.0%	9.1%
9	10	60.0%	20.0%	20.0%	0.0%	0.0%
10	6	83.3%	0.0%	16.7%	0.0%	0.0%
11	32	56.3%	31.3%	6.3%	0.0%	6.3%
12	55	50.9%	30.9%	3.6%	5.5%	9.1%
13	5	40.0%	40.0%	0.0%	0.0%	20.0%
14	7	71.4%	28.6%	0.0%	0.0%	0.0%
15	3	66.7%	33.3%	0.0%	0.0%	0.0%
20	1	0.0%	0.0%	100.0%	0.0%	0.0%
24	32	40.6%	46.9%	3.1%	3.1%	6.3%
25	45	60.0%	24.4%	11.1%	2.2%	2.2%
26	8	50.0%	37.5%	12.5%	0.0%	0.0%
27	1	0.0%	100.0%	0.0%	0.0%	0.0%
28	5	60.0%	40.0%	0.0%	0.0%	0.0%
29	27	55.6%	40.7%	3.7%	0.0%	0.0%
30	7	42.9%	28.6%	0.0%	0.0%	28.6%
31	24	75.0%	16.7%	0.0%	4.2%	4.2%
32	12	33.3%	41.7%	8.3%	8.3%	8.3%
33	83	32.5%	32.5%	18.1%	7.2%	9.6%
34	14	21.4%	42.9%	14.3%	14.3%	7.1%
36	1	100.0%	0.0%	0.0%	0.0%	0.0%

[1]On the survey the lowest response category was 0 – 24%. The 0% category was created from those who reported they did not see any modern equipment.

Table 75. Percent of Time Day Hikers Saw Landscape Modifications per Day, by Unit.

Unit	n	0%[1]	1 – 24%	25 – 49%	50 – 74%	75 – 100%
1	6	16.7%	33.3%	0.0%	0.0%	50.0%
2	1	0.0%	0.0%	0.0%	0.0%	100.0%
3	1	0.0%	100.0%	0.0%	0.0%	0.0%
4	5	40.0%	20.0%	20.0%	0.0%	20.0%
5	2	50.0%	0.0%	0.0%	50.0%	0.0%
6	22	22.7%	36.4%	22.7%	9.1%	9.1%
7	3	33.3%	33.3%	0.0%	0.0%	33.3%
8	11	54.5%	27.3%	0.0%	9.1%	9.1%
9	10	60.0%	20.0%	10.0%	0.0%	10.0%
10	6	33.3%	33.3%	16.7%	0.0%	16.7%
11	33	33.3%	36.4%	9.1%	6.1%	15.2%
12	55	40.0%	23.6%	3.6%	7.3%	25.5%
13	5	40.0%	60.0%	0.0%	0.0%	0.0%
14	7	14.3%	71.4%	0.0%	0.0%	14.3%
15	3	66.7%	0.0%	0.0%	0.0%	33.3%
20	1	100.0%	0.0%	0.0%	0.0%	0.0%
24	32	6.3%	43.8%	12.5%	12.5%	25.0%
25	45	6.7%	46.7%	11.1%	8.9%	26.7%
26	8	25.0%	75.0%	0.0%	0.0%	0.0%
27	1	0.0%	100.0%	0.0%	0.0%	0.0%
28	5	20.0%	80.0%	0.0%	0.0%	0.0%
29	27	48.1%	44.4%	3.7%	3.7%	0.0%
30	7	14.3%	28.6%	0.0%	28.6%	28.6%
31	25	36.0%	24.0%	12.0%	16.0%	12.0%
32	12	16.7%	66.7%	0.0%	0.0%	16.7%
33	82	20.7%	37.8%	11.0%	6.1%	24.4%
34	13	23.1%	15.4%	23.1%	30.8%	7.7%
36	1	0.0%	100.0%	0.0%	0.0%	0.0%

[1]On the survey the lowest response category was 0 – 24%. The 0% category was created from those who reported they did not see any landscape modifications.

Table 76. Percent of Time Day Hikers Saw other Park Visitors per Day, by Unit.

Unit	n	0%[1]	1 – 24%	25 – 49%	50 – 74%	75 – 100%
1	6	33.3%	50.0%	16.7%	0.0%	0.0%
2	1	0.0%	0.0%	0.0%	0.0%	100.0%
3	1	0.0%	0.0%	100.0%	0.0%	0.0%
4	6	16.7%	16.7%	33.3%	16.7%	16.7%
5	2	50.0%	50.0%	0.0%	0.0%	0.0%
6	22	40.9%	59.1%	0.0%	0.0%	0.0%
7	3	33.3%	33.3%	0.0%	33.3%	0.0%
8	10	40.0%	60.0%	0.0%	0.0%	0.0%
9	10	20.0%	80.0%	0.0%	0.0%	0.0%
10	6	50.0%	33.3%	16.7%	0.0%	0.0%
11	33	33.3%	57.6%	3.0%	6.1%	0.0%
12	55	14.5%	29.1%	16.4%	16.4%	23.6%
13	5	20.0%	60.0%	20.0%	0.0%	0.0%
14	7	14.3%	71.4%	14.3%	0.0%	0.0%
15	3	0.0%	100.0%	0.0%	0.0%	0.0%
20	1	0.0%	100.0%	0.0%	0.0%	0.0%
24	32	0.0%	34.4%	31.3%	25.0%	9.4%
25	43	2.3%	27.9%	23.3%	18.6%	27.9%
26	8	37.5%	12.5%	37.5%	0.0%	12.5%
27	1	100.0%	0.0%	0.0%	0.0%	0.0%
28	5	40.0%	40.0%	20.0%	0.0%	0.0%
29	26	38.5%	46.2%	7.7%	3.8%	3.8%
30	7	42.9%	14.3%	28.6%	0.0%	14.3%
31	25	32.0%	48.0%	16.0%	0.0%	4.0%
32	12	25.0%	58.3%	0.0%	16.7%	0.0%
33	82	12.2%	30.5%	17.1%	17.1%	23.2%
34	13	15.4%	23.1%	7.7%	30.8%	23.1%
36	1	0.0%	0.0%	100.0%	0.0%	0.0%

[1]On the survey the lowest response category was 0 – 24%. The 0% category was created from those who reported they did not see any other park visitors.

Interview Results

Interviews were conducted with 17 individuals; 13 were day hikers and 4 were backpackers. Given this distribution of interview respondents, it must be cautioned that interviews were more likely to capture the views of day hiker interviewees than backpackers. In addition, although interviews were conducted on randomly selected days, it is **not** a sample that represents all backcountry users. It is possible the views of those interviewed differ significantly from those not interviewed. In addition, interview results suggest there might be several different types of visitors with regard to views toward the backcountry. It is critical to note the responses to the interviews accurately reflect the view of the individual, and there are likely other visitors who share that view, however, the percentage of those with the same view (i.e., type of visitor) is not known.

The interview was semi-structured; a script was used, but the person conducting the interview could ask follow-up questions to clarify responses or to find out more information. The interview script is shown in Appendix B. The first question asked interviewees to distinguish among the indicators they felt had significant negative impacts on their experience and those that did not. As such, responses varied. However, the number of interviewees who mentioned a specific indicator provides some idea of which indicators were salient.

Fifteen of the interviews were conducted by Leah Roach and two by Peter Fix. Interviews were transcribed by Leah and read by the authors of this report. In a few instances during the back and forth exchange to build rapport between the interviewer and interviewee and in responses to clarify interviewee's questions, the interviewer inadvertently made statements that might have influenced responses. The authors of the report read through the interview transcript and both agreed on two responses that were removed due to potential bias. The second author conducted the initial coding of the interviews. Both authors then reviewed the coding, and adjustments in codes were made until consensus was reached.

Modern human use was given special attention in the survey as the backcountry management plan specifically stated the first survey conducted to monitor indicators would "evaluate the usefulness of this indicator and investigate other alternatives for indicating the impact of modern civilization on the wilderness experience" (National Park Service, 2006, pg. 40). Summaries of the comments related to factors that impact the experience in the backcountry are first presented below, followed by responses related to modern human use.

Factors Impacting the Backcountry Experience

Sound: Fifteen different respondents made 20 distinct comments related to motorized sound. These comments were placed into groups related to general motorized sounds (n = 10), airplanes (n = 5) and sounds from the park road (n = 5).

General Motorized Sound: Nine respondents made comments related to general motorized sound. Most interview respondents that commented on general motorized sound regarded it as something that should not be encountered in the backcountry because it detracts from the wilderness experience as well as the feeling of solitude. Some mentioned that, unless one hikes far into the park, hearing motorized sound is inevitable so it only becomes an issue when it is excessive. Others mentioned that, to them, the purpose of hiking in DNP as opposed to other areas of Alaska or the lower 48 is to get away from motorized sound in the backcountry.

Park Road: Noise from the park road corridor was mentioned by five respondents. Perceptions of noise traveling from the park road into the backcountry varied, as some respondents said they left the noise of the road as they hiked a half-mile into the backcountry and/or gained elevation, while others said they did not lose the noise of the park road and it actually worsened with gains in elevation. In general, those interviewed that heard the noise of the park road during their hike did not mind such noise because they knew they would be hiking near the road and motorized sound was expected.

Airplanes: Sound from airplanes was mentioned by four respondents. Several interviewees commented that the sound of planes flying overhead detracted from their backcountry experience, but many agreed that air traffic was necessary and should be closely monitored and controlled so as to limit the negative effect on hikers. Limiting the number of flights or flying hours, setting limits on altitude, or designating flying zones to prevent planes from flying between the park entrance and Denali were all suggested as ideas for lessening the impact of air traffic on hikers.

Modern Equipment: Fifteen respondents made 26 distinct comments relating to modern equipment, with four categories emerging: general (n = 12), research equipment (n = 7), heavy equipment/construction (n = 5), and motorized equipment (n = 2).

General Modern Equipment: Eleven respondents made general comments regarding modern equipment. They generally implied that modern equipment has a negative impact on their backcountry experience, but it is tolerated in areas where they expect to encounter it, such as near the road. Some hikers choose DNP because they don't expect to encounter modern equipment in the backcountry like they would in other parts of Alaska or the lower 48. The biggest concerns about modern equipment were when it detracted from the scenery or produced sound. One respondent mentioned a concern with things that are left by maintenance or research crews that use modern equipment. Modern equipment used for maintenance or for improving park access was understood and was not a bother for most respondents that commented on it.

Research Equipment: Six respondents made comments about research equipment. Virtually all respondents who made comments about research equipment showed ambivalence towards encountering research equipment in the backcountry, with one noting that ongoing research within the park is a positive thing. One respondent commented that research equipment would have a negative impact if there were excessive amounts of it, such as "if every single hill top had a weather reporting station on it." It was a common belief that research equipment should be fairly unnoticeable.

Heavy Equipment/construction: Five respondents made comments related to heavy equipment and/or construction. Heavy equipment working within the park was generally seen as having a negative impact on the experience of interviewees, even when it was understood to be necessary for road maintenance, gravel extraction, etc. Noise from heavy equipment was noted to be particularly negative.

Motorized Equipment: Two respondents made comments related to motorized equipment. Respondents that commented on motorized equipment specified that they did not expect to encounter it in the backcountry. One respondent noted that they would prefer not to encounter motorized equipment, but understands the need for such equipment at times.

Landscape Modifications: Eleven respondents made 22 distinct comments regarding landscape modifications. These comments can be categorized into general comments (n = 5), trails (n = 10), markers/storage (n = 4) and the road (n = 3).

General Comments Regarding Landscape Modifications: Nine respondents made general comments regarding landscape modifications. There were several views regarding the impacts of landscape modifications. Some expressed difficulty in knowing what constitutes a landscape modification. These comments were more involved than an animal vs. human caused trail, raising issues of human caused climate change and acid rain. Some viewed landscape modifications as positive because they increased the hiker's ability to enjoy the park. Others thought landscape modifications were necessary, but undesirable. The importance of landscape modifications was understood, and thus landscape modifications are tolerated to a certain extent, but the general preference was not to encounter them in the backcountry.

Trails: Ten respondents made comments regarding trails. Social trails were generally seen as having a negative impact on the backcountry experience due to aesthetics and concerns over resource impacts, and efforts to curtail the use of such trails was seen as positive. Some respondents appreciated trails for making travel in the backcountry easier. Maintained trails in high-use areas and near the road were acceptable, and several mentioned trails along the road corridor could co-exist with a trailless backcountry. One respondent was very adamant that there should be more established day-hike trails and more accommodation for hikers that would be interested in hiking eight or ten-mile loops, for example.

Markers/Storage: Four respondents made comments regarding markers/storage. Most comments regarding markers or storage mentioned that in high-traffic areas, such as near the road or on established trails they are necessary and/or expected and therefore acceptable and even helpful. In excess, and especially farther out in the backcountry, these forms of landscape modification were said to be negative.

Road: Three respondents made comments relating to the park road. One respondent mentioned that seeing the Toklat bridge throughout their hike had a negative impact while another group of hikers chose not to leave sight of the park road for orienteering purposes. One interviewee mentioned that more roads would not cause a negative impact on the experience because they would provide more access.

Other Visitors and Large Groups: Sixteen respondents made 22 different comments about other visitors. Most respondents felt that occasional contacts with other hikers had no negative effect on the backcountry experience as they had just as much right to enjoy the park as everyone else, although a couple of comments noted that seeing other people made it feel less like wilderness. However, most of these comments also mentioned groups of six or more would have a negative impact on their experience; i.e., encounters with solo hikers or small groups are tolerated, encounters with large groups are not. One respondent mentioned that exchanging stories with other hikers they encountered can provide a positive impact on their experience. Noise and irresponsible behavior from other hikers were mentioned as causes of negative impacts.

Litter and Human Waste: Thirteen respondents made 14 comments about litter and human waste. Virtually all respondents declared that litter and human waste have a strong negative impact on the backcountry experience. Comments mentioned that leaving litter and human waste in the backcountry is irresponsible and visitors have an obligation to practice "leave no trace."

Responses Related to Modern Human Use
The responses to the questions regarding modern human use revealed interesting insight into the interviewees' perceptions on the subject. It is important to note many of the interviews were conducted with day hikers. Many of the respondents associated modern human use with the road corridor, and especially access into the park, including two of the backpackers in the sample. Interviewees noted little evidence of modern human use originating from outside the road corridor, and it likely follows for this reason that aspect of modern human use, e.g., research equipment in the field, was not salient. Respondents indicated it was good to monitor impacts of modern human use. However, it appears the road corridor, and the impacts associated with it, dominate other evidence of modern human use when one is in the backcountry. While the interview did not explicitly instruct the respondent to exclude the road corridor, the high degree of salience of impacts associated with the road corridor illustrate that it will be challenging to ask respondents about impacts of modern human use that originate outside the road corridor. It probably will not make much sense to visitors if they are asked only about encountering a piece of equipment such as an automated weather station when the park road and buses have been visible during their hike. However, excluding impacts originating in the park road corridor from modern human use would be more appropriate for overnight backpackers once they were well outside of the road corridor.

Summaries of responses to the different questions regarding impacts of modern human use are listed below.

Impacts of Modern Human Use: Eleven interviewees commented on the impacts of modern human use. Eielson Visitor Center was listed as having a positive impact on one hiker's experience because of the building's unique design and integration into the landscape. More respondents saw the impacts of modern human use as being neutral or positive rather than negative, mostly because it contributed to access and the ability to experience the park. This view was also expressed by two backpackers in the sample. From these comments it appears the interviewees associated modern human use with things along the road corridor. In addition, the interviewees did not see much evidence of impacts of modern human use outside of road corridor. It is important to note the interviews consisted primarily of day hikers. One respondent said that modern human use had a negative impact on their [groups] experience because they were not accustomed to so many people and facilities within a park.

Importance of Monitoring Modern human Use: The question asking about the importance of monitoring modern use was asked as a follow-up question if the importance of monitoring, or lack of, was not evident in the response to the question asking about the impacts of modern human use. Four interviewees provided additional information on the importance of monitoring modern human use and all agreed that it was important, even necessary.

Adequate Measure of Impacts of Modern Human Use: Eight interviewees provided responses related to whether monitoring encounters with modern equipment was an adequate measure of the impacts of modern human use. It was a general consensus that monitoring encounters with modern equipment and landscape modifications with a visitor survey was an adequate measure of impacts of modern human use on the backcountry experience. One comment was made that monitoring park visitors was a necessary component as well.

Other Factors Related to Modern Human Use: Seven respondents made comments regarding other factors related to modern human use. Three were vague without offering specific suggestions. Two respondents mentioned to keep impacts of modern human use to a minimum, with one of them acknowledging a balance between minimizing impacts and a need for access. One respondent mentioned a need for monitoring backcountry campsites to ensure campers are taking proper care of the area. One group felt that there should be better guidance and preparation for beginner backpackers.

Importance of Monitoring Indicators: Fourteen respondents made 16 comments regarding the importance of monitoring indicators. Most respondents felt that it is important to monitor the indicators, with particular emphasis on monitoring and managing park visitors and large groups. One respondent mentioned that large groups should not be monitored because the group participants are experiencing a positive impact by being in the group, despite a negative impact on the backcountry experience for other hikers, and one cannot prioritize the impacts on certain hikers over others. Modern equipment, motorized sound, and human waste were all mentioned as important to monitor as well, but were not mentioned as frequently as park visitors. Landscape modifications were mentioned as important to monitor for proper maintenance.

Comments Written on Survey

The backpacker survey had a section in which people could write in comments related to factors important to their experience in Denali National Park. Many respondents wrote in responses. Although the day hiker survey did not have a section for comments, several respondents made comments. As respondents were not prompted to comment on any particular topic, these responses are a good indication of issues that were salient to those backpackers and day hikers who responded. However, it must be noted these comments do not represent all backcountry visitors.

The majority of the comments related to rangers, both in general and at the BIC, and information provided. The majority of these comments were positive, although there were some negative comments and suggestions. The second largest category related to airplanes, with a strong majority being negative (Table 77). The comments are listed in Appendix D. Those who made negative or mixed comments regarding airplanes reported on average 5.2 motorized sound encounters (across 71 days of hiking) compared to 2.9 reported encounters from those who did not make negative comments(across 454 days of hiking) (t [454, 71]= -3.18, p = 0.002).

Table 77. Number of and Categories of Comments Written on Survey

Category	Number of comments	Number positive	Number neutral	Number mixed[1]	Number negative	Number of suggestions
Rangers/BIC/info	41	24	5	0	9	5
Airplanes	17	0	3	2	12	0
Buses	9	2	1	0	4	3
Other visitors	9	3[2]	5	0	2	0
Trails	5	2[3]	2	0	1	0
Landscape modifications	4	2	2	0	0	0
Access	2	0	0	0	2	0
Park road	2	0	0	0	2	0
Litter/human waste	2	0	2	0	0	0
Motorized sound (general)	1	0	1	0	0	0
Camping out of sight/sound of others	1	0	1	0	0	0
Modern human use	2	0	2	0	0	0

[1]Mixed refers to a neutral and negative statements being present.
[2]Positive toward limiting visitor numbers.
[3]The positive comments were regarding the lack of trails.

Discussion/Conclusion

The level of eight indicators of resource and social conditions experienced by backpackers and seven experienced by day hikers was measured in summer of 2010. With respect to whether the standards were violated, the type of comparison between the indicator and standard makes a large difference in how often the standards were violated. Comparing the mean level of the indicator to the standard is least stringent comparison as it is allows several individuals to report levels above the standard, yet still be in compliance. Comparing the indicators to the standards with the criteria that the standard is violated if at least one individual experiences conditions above the standard (i.e., "zero tolerance") is a significantly more rigorous comparison.

For backpackers, when comparing the mean level of the indicators to the standard, motorized sound and landscape modifications had many units above the mean. The other indicators had relatively few units above the mean. When comparing the indicators to the standards with zero tolerance, motorized sound, encountering modern equipment, encountering landscape modifications, and seeing litter or human waste had a majority of units that violated the standards and for encountering other park visitors the standard was violated in 38% of the units. In addition, the standard for motorized sound and encountering landscape modifications was violated the majority of days, 85% and 93% respectively. The standard for encountering modern equipment was violated on half of the days, encountering other park visitors was violated on 24% of days, and seeing litter and human waste was violated 43% of days.

The indicators of motorized sound and encountering landscape modifications appear out of compliance for backpackers as all analyses showed that the standards were often violated. However, it must be noted that impacts from the road corridor were not excluded from the survey responses. This increased the occurrence of the indicators, however, the magnitude of the effect cannot be determined. Modern equipment and encounters with other visitors should be carefully monitored as under a policy of zero tolerance there were a high number of units and days above the standard. Likewise, litter and human waste, when comparing the indicator to the standard under the condition of zero tolerance, exhibited a relatively high level of units and days above the standard.

The standard for camping out of sight or sound of others was violated on 32 nights, which puts it in violation of the standard. It should be noted the survey did not measure if a backpacker's first choice of campsite was not available. As campsites are self chosen, perhaps additional emphasis on camping out of sight or sound of others in the backcountry permit orientation would be useful.

For day hikers, when comparing the mean level of the indicators to the standard, motorized sound and encounters with landscape modifications had a high number of units above the standard. Encounters with other park visitors had a relatively low number of units above the standard, and encountering large groups and NPS personnel and seeing litter or human waste had few units above the standard. When comparing the indicators to the standards with zero tolerance, for all indicators except for encounters with large groups, the standards were violated for the majority of units and days.

The indicators of motorized sound, encountering landscape modifications, and encountering other park visitors appear out of compliance. Under the criteria of zero tolerance all indicators except for encounters with large groups appear to be exceeded.

Recommendations

Criteria of good standards states the standard should be expressed as a percent, e.g., "encounter no more than two other visitors on 90% of the days from June 1 to August 31." This allows tolerance for high use or peak days in which it might be inevitable that the standards will be violated. This should be considered in revisions to the standards.

A criteria for good indicators is that they are easily measured. Two of the indicators, encounters with landscape modifications and encounters with modern equipment, are difficult to explain to visitors. For example, visitors need to know animal trails are not included in landscape modifications, yet this is a difficult distinction to make. Visitors also need to know what types of equipment are included in modern equipment. Definitions of these indicators should be refined so it is easier for the visitors to understand what is meant by the indicator.

Currently, if a visitor reported seeing litter and/or human waste, it is not possible to know if they saw litter or human waste. As these two items would have different messages during the backcountry permit orientation, it would be beneficial to know which to emphasize. This could be achieved either through separate indicators for litter and human waste or simply asking separate questions for litter and human waste. As the standard was expressed "no more than 5% seeing litter and human waste," the survey only measured whether the visitor saw litter and/or human waste or not. However, future studies might also measure the frequency in which visitors saw litter and/or human waste.

The motorized sound indicator consists of airplanes and other motorized sounds. The issues revolving around overflights make it desirable to know with certainty whether instances of the visitor hearing motorized sound is attributable to airplanes or some other source. While different indicators might not be desirable for the different sources of motorized sound, separate questions to measure the source of different motorized sounds would be desirable.

The opportunity to camp out of site or sound indicator includes in the description "…however, visitors may still choose to camp where they can see or hear others." This needs to be refined. The visitors choosing to camp in site of another visitor impacts the other visitor's ability to camp out of sight or sound. The policy, and corresponding standard, needs to be consistent that visitors must camp out of sight or sound of others.

The survey used in this study included the road corridor and many impacts originated from the road corridor as indicated by survey respondents. As impacts from the road corridor impact the backcountry experience, it is recommended the standards include these impacts. In addition, it is difficult for the respondent to know which impacts originated from within the road corridor and which from outside of the road corridor.

The indicator for camping was difficult to measure. Given the nature of camping, it occurs over two "days." While other campers might not be visible in the evening, another group could set up camp within sight or sound during the evening. The timing of when to ask about the impacts of camping is difficult as camping impacts need to be linked to a specific date and unit. If respondents fill out the survey each evening they could report camping impacts for the campsite starting the previous night and ending in the morning, or they could report camping impacts for the campsite that evening. The survey used in this study instructed people to fill out the survey in the morning and to mark the date and time of the period for which they were reporting. However, some may have found this confusing. An alternative would be to instruct people to complete the survey each evening and just record the date, being certain to link the correct date and unit to the night of camping. The camping impact could be adjusted later if their ability to camp out of sight or sound of others changed after they answered the question (i.e., if someone set up camp within sight after they answered the question, they can edit their survey).

As discussed earlier in the report, based on feedback from park staff the questions measuring the importance of the indictors were changed prior to the administration of the survey. The questions included on the final survey proved to be confusing. Future research should use the original version which is as follows. The definition of "low level" was taken from the backcountry management plan.

Rate the importance of a low level of each of the following (a "low level" is defined after each item)

Importance of a **low level** of:	Not at all	Somewhat	Moderately	Extremely
Motorized sound (*1 encounter per day*)	1	2	3	4
Modern equipment (*1 encounter per trip*)	1	2	3	4
Landscape modifications (*no encounters*)	1	2	3	4
Park visitors (*no encounters*)	1	2	3	4
Groups of six or more visitors (*no encounters*)	1	2	3	4
Toilet paper or human waste (*no encounters*)	1	2	3	4
The ability to camp out of sight or sound of others (*always*)	1	2	3	4

The area of the park covered by the OP1 management prescription is extremely large, starting 150 feet from the park road to areas that require several days to reach by hiking. Yet, the standards are the same across the entire area. This implies visitor densities are consistent across these areas and visitors are homogenous. The interviews suggest there might be different types of visitors present, e.g., one type of visitor could be someone with limited backcountry experience taking a bus trip into the park and desiring to take a short hike into the backcountry, but not necessarily feeling comfortable being completely separated from others. This might contrast with the experienced backcountry user that seeks to take a multi-day trip and not see other individuals. Yet, both of these visitors would be hiking in an area with the same management prescription. Perhaps different zones close to the road corridor, with different standards, can better capture the diversity of visitors in the park.

Further, the definition of indicators and standards used in the Denali BCMP, "specific, measurable physical, ecological, or social variable that reflect the overall condition of a zone" and minimum acceptable condition for each indicator variable," respectively, stem from a carrying capacity perspective (National Park Service 2005). As such they tend to focus on defining when an impact becomes too great. Other management frameworks such as Experienced Based Management (Manfredo 2002) and Outcomes Focused Management (Driver 2009) also focus on impacts to avoid, but in addition focus on positive, desirable outcomes. An alternative definition of indicators and standards that follows this philosophy defines an indicator as "the biophysical, social, managerial, or other condition that managers and visitors care about for a given experience" and suggests standards should "identify conditions that are desirable as well as conditions that managers don't want to exceed" (Vaske et al. 2002). Principles from the Experienced Based Management approach would seek to identify different users and create zones, with appropriate indicators and standards, to match their desired experiences. For example, there might be a small zone that is frequented by day hikers with indicators that relate more to experiencing unique ecosystems and feeling in touch with the park as opposed to encounters with others and modern equipment.

Literature Cited

Driver, B. L., editor. 2008. Managing to optimize the beneficial outcomes of recreation. State College, PA, Venture Publishing, Inc.

Manfredo, M. J., editor. 2002. Wildlife viewing: a management handbook. Corvallis, OR, Oregon State University Press.

National Park Service. n.d. Backcountry Management Plan: Denali National Park. Denali National Park and Preserve, Denali Park, Alaska, U.S. Department of the Interior.

National Park Service. 2005. Denali National Park and Preserve revised draft backcountry management plan. General management plan amendment and environmental impact statement. April 2005. Denali National Park and Preserve, Denali Park, Alaska, U.S. Department of the Interior.

National Park Service. 2006. Denali National Park Final Backcountry Management Plan. General Management Plan Amendment and Environmental Impact Statement January 2006. Denali Park, Alaska,U.S. Department of the Interior.

Vaske, J. J. 2008. Survey Research and Analysis: Applications in Parks, Recreation and Human Dimensions. State College, PA, Venture Publishing, Inc.

Vaske, J. J., D. Whittaker, B. Shelby, and M. J. Manfredo. 2002. Indicators and standards: developing definitions of quality. M. J. Manfredo, editor, Wildlife viewing: a management handbook. Corvallis, OR, Oregon State University Press.

Appendix A. Management Areas and Standards

Source: National Park Service 2005, pg 32 "Table 1: Management Area Descriptions"

Management Area	Purpose	Resource Conditions				
		Trails and Campsite Disturbance	**Evidence of modern Human Use** *max. Encounters/day*	**Landscape Modifications** *allowed to mitigate for visitor use?*	**Litter & Human Waste** *max. % of visitors who encounter*	**Natural Sound Disturbance**
A	Provide a diversity of opportunities for wilderness recreational activities that are relatively accessible to day-users and to those who have limited wilderness travel skills or equipment	**Medium** Occasional social trails, campsites	**Medium** 3 encounters/day	No	**Low** *5%*	**High** max % aud/hr: 25 max #/day : 25 max dBA: 60
B	Provide opportunities for wilderness recreational activities suitable for day-users and overnight users that are remote and require self-reliance	**Low** Few if any social trails, campsites	**Low** 1 encounters/day	No	**Low** *5%*	**Medium** max % aud/hr: 15 max #/day : 10 max dBA: 40
C	Provide opportunities for climbing and mountaineering experiences in a wilderness setting	**Medium** Occasional social trails, campsites	**Medium** 3 encounters/day	No	**Low** *5%*	**Medium** max % aud/hr: 15 max #/day : 10 max dBA: 40
D	Provide opportunities for extended expeditions that are remote self-reliance, significant time commitment, and thorough advance planning	**Low** Few if any social trails, campsites	**Low** 1 encounters/day	No	**Low** *5%*	**Low** max % aud/hr: 5 max #/day : 1 max dBA: 40
Portal	Provide high-use airplane landing areas that provide access to remote parts of the park and preserve Year-round or seasonal	N/A	**Medium** 3 encounters/day	No	**Low** *5%*	Same as for surrounding area, but no lower than Medium
Portal – Major Landing Areas	Provide a diversity of opportunities for wilderness recreational activities that are relatively accessible to day-users and to those who have limited wilderness travel skills or equipment	N/A	**High** 5 encounters/day	Yes	**Low** *5%*	**Very High** max % aud/hr: 50 max #/day : 50 max dBA: 60
Corridor	Provide high-use airplane landing areas that are suitable for both day use and expedition drop-off and pick-up Seasonal, May-September	**Medium** Occasional social trails, campsites	**High** 5 encounters/day	Yes	**Low** *5%*	**High** max % aud/hr: 25 max #/day : 10 max dBA: 60
Back Country Hiker	Provide day use trails into the backcountry in areas that are accessible to many visitors Year-round or seasonal	N/A	**High** 5 encounters/day	Yes	**Low** *5%*	**Medium** max % aud/hr: 15 max #/day : 10 max dBA: 40
Ruth Glacier Special Use	Provide for high use of transportation services during the season when large numbers of day use accessing the Ruth Amphitheater Seasonal, (SIC)	**Medium** Occasional social trails, campsites	**Medium** 3 encounters/day	No	**Low** *5%*	**Very High** max % aud/hr: 50 max #/day : 50 max dBA: 60
OP1	Provide opportunities for day use and overnight wilderness recreation activities that are remote and require self-reliance in an area that has limited opportunities for motorized access	**Medium** Occasional social trails, campsites	**Low** 1 encounters/day	No	**Low** *5%*	**Low** max % aud/hr: 5 max #/day : 1 max dBA: 40
OP2	Provide opportunities for extended expeditions that are remote and require a high degree of self-reliance, significant time commitment, and thorough advance planning in an area that has limited opportunities for motorized access	**Low** Few if any social trails, campsites	**Low** 1 encounters/day	No	**Low** *5%*	**Low** max % aud/hr: 5 max #/day : 1 max dBA: 40
West Buttress Special Use	Provide seasonal route to the summit of Mount McKinley that can accommodate large numbers of climbers during the primary climbing season Seasonal, late April to mid-July	N/A	**High** 5 encounters/day	Yes	**Low** *5%*	**Low** max % aud/hr: 5 max #/day : 1 max dBA: 40

Old Park

103

Management Area	Purpose	Social Conditions				
		Encounters with People *max. parties encountered/day*	Encounters With Large Groups *encounters possible?*	Camping Density *able to camp out of sight & sound (s&s) of others?*	Accessibility	Administrative Presence
A	Provide a diversity of opportunities for wilderness recreational activities that are relatively accessible to day-users and to those who have limited wilderness travel skills or equipment	**High** 5 encounters/day	Yes	**Low** always able to camp out of s&s	**Medium**	**Medium** routine visitor contacts
B	Provide opportunities for wilderness recreational activities suitable for day-users and overnight users that are remote and require self-reliance	**Medium** 3 encounters/day	Yes	**Low** always able to camp out of s&s	**Low-Medium**	**Low** occasional patrols
C	Provide opportunities for climbing and mountaineering experiences in a wilderness setting	**High** 5 encounters/day	Yes	**Low** always able to camp out of s&s	**Low-Very Low**	**Low** occasional patrols
D	Provide opportunities for extended expeditions that are remote self-reliance, significant time commitment, and thorough advance planning	**Low** unlikely to encounter other parties	No	**Low** always able to camp out of s&s	**Low**	**Low** occasional patrols
Portal	Provide high-use airplane landing areas that provide access to remote parts of the park and preserve Year-round or seasonal	N/A	Yes	**Medium** may have to camp in s&s during peak season	**Medium**	**Medium** routine visitor contacts
Portal – Major Landing Areas	Provide a diversity of opportunities for wilderness recreational activities that are relatively accessible to day-users and to those who have limited wilderness travel skills or equipment	N/A	Yes	**High** little or no opportunity to camp out of s&s	**High**	**Medium-High** routine visitor contacts – frequently present
Corridor	Provide high-use airplane landing areas that are suitable for both day use and expedition drop-off and pick-up Seasonal, May-September	**Very High** 10 encounters/day	Yes	**Medium** may have to camp in s&s during peak season	**Low-High**	**Medium** routine visitor contacts
Back Country Hiker	Provide day use trails into the backcountry in areas that are accessible to many visitors Year-round or seasonal	**Very High** 10 encounters/day	Yes	**N/A** No camping allowed on trails	**High**	**High** frequently present
Ruth Glacier Special Use	Provide for high use of transportation services during the season when large numbers of day use accessing the Ruth Amphitheater Seasonal, [SIC]	**High** 5 encounters/day	Yes	**Low** always able to camp out of s&s	**Low-Very Low**	**Medium** routine visitor contacts
OP1	Provide opportunities for day use and overnight wilderness recreation activities that are remote and require self-reliance in an area that has limited opportunities for motorized access	**Medium** 3 encounters/day	Yes	**Low** always able to camp out of s&s	**Medium-High**	**Medium** routine visitor contacts
OP2	Provide opportunities for extended expeditions that are remote and require a high degree of self-reliance, significant time commitment, and thorough advance planning in an area that has limited opportunities for motorized access	**Low** unlikely to encounter other parties	No	**Low** always able to camp out of s&s	**Low**	**Low** occasional patrols
West Buttress Special Use	Provide seasonal route to the summit of Mount McKinley that can accommodate large numbers of climbers during the primary climbing season Seasonal, late April to mid-July	N/A	Yes	**High** little or no opportunity to camp out of s&s	**Low-Very Low**	**High** frequently present

Old Park

Resource Conditions				
Trails and Campsite Disturbance	**Evidence of modern Human Use**	**Landscape Modifications**	**Litter & Human Waste**	**Natural Sound Disturbance**
		Yes There may be visible mitigations for visitors use such as constructed trail segments, route markers, signs, bridges, designated campsites, food storage facilities, sanitation facilities, fixed climbing lines, or others as described or proposed by this plan	**Low** No more than 5% of visitors encounter human waste, toilet paper, or litter in the backcountry	**Very High** Natural sounds are often interrupted by motorized noise including loud noise Motorized noise may be audible up to 50% of any hour, and there may be up to 50 motorized noise intrusions per day that exceed natural ambient sound Motorized noise does not exceed 60dBA
	High Visitors have at most 5 encounters with modern equipment or landscape modifications each day of their trip	**No** There are no visible landscape mitigations for visitor use		**High** Natural sounds are often interrupted by motorized noise including loud noise Motorized noise may be audible up to 25% of any hour, and there may be as many as 25 motorized noise intrusions per day that exceed natural ambient sound Motorized noise does not exceed 60dBA
Medium Visitors notice occasional social trails, campsites, or cut or broken vegetation	**Medium** Visitors have at most 3 encounters with modern equipment or landscape modifications each day of their trip			**Medium** Natural sounds predominate in this area, but there are infrequent motorized intrusions, a few of which may be loud Motorized noise may be audible up to 15% of any hour, and there may be as many as 10 motorized noise intrusions per day that exceed natural ambient sound Motorized noise does not exceed 60dBA
Low Visitors notice few if any signs of social trails, campsites, or cut or broken vegetation	**Low** Visitors have at most 1 encounters per trip with modern equipment or landscape modifications			**Low** Natural sounds predominate in this area and motorized noise intrusions are very rare and usually faint Motorized noise may be audible up to 5% of any hour, and there is no more that 1 motorized intrusion per day that exceeds natural ambient sound Motorized noise does not exceed 40dBA
N/A Identifies an alpine area that has very scarce or no vegetation or soil Trails and campsites on snow are not monitored				
Notes The "Medium" descriptor is intended to match current conditions in the Old Park in areas accessible from the road corridor The first phase of the monitoring program will utilize existing data and new field observations to describe those conditions in more detail	**Notes** "Modern equipment" includes communication facilities, chain saws, motorized or mechanized vehicles, on the ground, and other similar devices This definition does not include portable devices that a person could reasonably carry without assistance (e g , cell phones, GPS units, fuel-burning stoves), subsistence equipment such as traps or firearms, or aircraft in flight An "encounter" refers to a visual recognition A single trail or route markers associated with a single route will count as only one encounter Audio recognition of noise is covered under the National Sound Disturbance standards	**Notes** "Landscape modifications" specifically do not include historic or cultural resources such as historic cabins, gravesites, or other structures or artifacts They also do not include permitted modifications for subsistence use such as cabins or trap line trails		**Notes** "Audible" means audibility to a person on normal hearing Maximum sound levels assume the measurement device is more than 50 feet for the noise source For comparison, 40dBA is the overall sound level inside a typical residential home 70dBA is the sound level of a vacuum cleaner as perceived user

Cont:
Source: National Park Service 2005, pg 33 "Table 2: Key to the Management Area Descriptors"

Social Conditions				
Encounters with People	**Encounters With Large Groups**	**Camping Density**	**Accessibility**	**Administrative Presence**
Very High Visitors commonly encounter other parties in these areas They generally encounter 10 or fewer parties per day	**Yes** 1 or 2 of the parties encountered may have more than 6 people			
High Visitors commonly encounter other parties in these areas, although they still have many opportunities to be alone They generally encounter 5 or fewer parties per day	**No** No parties are encountered that are larger than 6 people	**High** During the season of peak visitation, there is little or no opportunity for visitors to camp out of sight or sound of others At other times of year visitors may be able to camp out of sight and sound of others	**High** These areas are suitable for casual use and do not require extensive time commitments, specialized backcountry travel skills, advance planning, or self-reliance	**High** Rangers are frequently present, so visitors generally have some contact with them Visitors may occasionally encounter stag got permitted researchers involved in inventory and monitoring projects and research in some areas
Medium Visitors occasionally encounter other parties in these areas, but are almost always alone They are generally encounter 2 or fewer parties per day		**Medium** During the season of peak visitation may have to camp within sight or sound of others, but often are able to avoid doing so At other times of the year visitors generally are able to camp out of sight and sound	**Medium** Visits to these areas require self-reliance, but may not require extensive time commitments, some specialized skills or extensive advance planning	**Medium** Rangers may make routine visitor contacts, so visitors may be aware of administrative presence Visitors may occasionally encounter staff or permitted researchers involved in inventory and monitoring projects and research in some areas
Low Visitors are unlikely to encounter other parties in these areas during the course of their backcountry trip		**Low** Visitors always able to camp out of sight and sound	**Low** Visits to these areas require significant time commitment, specialized backcountry travel skills, advance planning, and high-degree of self-reliance	**Low** Administrative presence is generally limited to emergency activities and occasional patrols, with research and resource projects in some areas
N/A There is no standard for encounter rate in this area Visitors may always be within sight or sound of other visitors		**N/A** No camping will be allowed on the trails	**Very Low** Visits to these areas require significant time commitment, specialized back country skills, thorough advance planning, and a high degree of self-reliance	
Notes An encounter is the unaided recognition by sight or sound of another park user, including other recreationalists or subsistence users An encounter does not include aircraft in flight which are addressed under Natural Sound Disturbance		**Notes** This category refers only to opportunity to camp outside of sight or sound of other park visitors however, visitors may still choose to camp where they can see or hear others "Sight or sound" refers to unaided recognition of another campsite from the site where the visitor camps for the night	**Notes** NPS management largely determines the degree of accessibility by providing facilities (such as trails) or services (transportation, guide services) that determine how easy or difficult it is to travel in an area of the park Terrain also plays a role, primarily in the alpine mountaineering areas that require specialized equipment and knowledge These are the only areas that achieve a "very low" rating, although the availability of guide services that can provide equipment and instruction can boost the rating to a "low " Areas accessible to day visitors who decide to visit spontaneously without planning or preparation achieve a "high" rating	**Notes** This category only includes interactions with administrative and research personnel, which are not included with the encounter rate standards given above Interactions with park aircraft, research equipment, snowmachines, or other equipment, and included in the standards for Evidence of Modern Human Use and Natural Sound Disturbance

Source: National Park Service 2005, pg 34 "Table 3: Monitoring and Process for Evaluation"

Indicator	Monitoring	Process for Evaluation
Trail & Campsite Disturbance	Monitoring will occur at three levels. These include: 1) the use of an existing grid system of plots for monitoring changes in vegetation cover that are randomly distributed through the park and preserve. 2) a set of index sited the known social trail or campsite formation can be monitored, and 3) a random sample of additional locations selected each year. Variables to monitor will include bare ground, vegetation cover, soil compaction, physical damage to plants, and site characteristics, such as soil moisture and soil temperature.	The "Medium" descriptor is intended to match current conditions in the Old Park in areas accessible for the park road corridor. The first phase of the monitoring program will utilize existing data and new field observations to describe those conditions in more detail.
Evidence of modern Human Use and Landscape Modifications	Monitoring will be conducted at least once every five years by visitor survey, and will be supplemented by continuous observation or ranger patrols.	The first visitor survey after plan approval will contain questions to evaluate the usefulness of this indicator and investigate other alternatives for indicating the impact of modern civilization on the wilderness experience. Survey results could be used to modify this indicator, but the relative differences between categories (High, Medium. Low) will be retained.
Litter & Human Waste	Monitoring will be conducted at least once every five years by survey of backcountry visitors. This information will be supplemented by the observations of park staff during backcountry patrols.	
Natural Sound Disturbance	Sound monitoring will be conducted on a continuous basis using remote monitors. Long-term monitoring will take place at locations of particular concern or where it has been determined that management action is necessary to meet standards. Other locations will be randomly sampled.	Indicators and standards will be used as benchmarks for five years while additional information is gathered through the initial stages of the monitoring program. After five years, the NPS will propose changes to either the indicators of standards through a public process. Relative differences between categories Low, Medium, High, Very High) will be retained during the revision process.
Encounters with People and Large Groups	Monitoring will be conducted at least once every five years by survey of backcountry visitors and "displaced" backcountry visitors. This information will be supplemented by the observations of park staff during backcountry patrols. "Displaced" backcountry visitors are those who will visit the park backcountry, but do not because of management limitations, crowding, or other factors make it an undesirable destination.	The NPS will review encounter rate standards after each five-year survey to evaluate visitor satisfaction and the success of standards in achieving management area goals. If professional judgment suggests that changes are necessary, the NPS will propose new indicators and/or standards through a public process. The relative differences between management areas will be retained.
Camping Density	Monitoring will be conducted at least once every five years by survey of backcountry visitors. This information will be supplemented by the observations of park staff during backcountry patrols.	As part of the monitoring process, NPS will evaluate the importance placed by the park users on this indicator. The distinctions between categories could be adjusted through a public process within the context of all the indicators related to "social conditions" in the park backcountry.
Accessibility	This category is descriptive only. The actions that determine the rating are listed elsewhere in this plan. Since the status will not change without additional action, monitoring in unnecessary.	
Administrative Presence	Ranger patrols will record and report visitor contacts. Visitor surveys will assess the amount and quality of interactions between visitors and NPS rangers and researchers at least once every five years.	There are no specific quantitative indicators of standards proposed for this category.

Appendix B: Survey Instruments

The day hiker survey is shown on pages 110 to 111, the backpacker survey is shown on pages 112 to 115, and the semi-structured interview guide is on pages 116 to 117. The backpacker survey was eight pages. Pages three through seven repeat the questions from page two. For space considerations pages three through seven are not shown.

The survey shown in this appendix was the version used throughout the second half of the summer, which contained clarification that landscape modifications included "constructed and human caused trails" and included the instructions to "Do not include animal trails." The survey used in the first half of the summer did not include that cause. See page 24 for a discussion of a comparison of the two versions of the survey.

The actually surveys had minimal margins. The surveys contained in this appendix are pdf versions of the original surveys that have been slightly reduced in size to fit the formatting of the report. Because of the reduction, the text of the survey appears slightly blurry. However, the printed version did not have blurry text.

Denali National Park Backcountry Day User Survey

We are interested in your hike or walk into the backcountry, which is defined as anything 150 feet (45 meters) or farther from the park road and parking areas. Please use this survey to describe your experiences in the backcountry.

Use the map below and the larger map on the easel to identify the backcountry unit (or units) in which you hiked. The University of Alaska Fairbanks (UAF) researcher can assist you in identifying the unit(s) in which you hiked. The backcountry units are the numbers inside the white circles. The park entrance (east) is on the right hand side of the map and Wonder Lake and Kantishna (west) are on the left hand side of the map. After identifying the backcountry unit in which you hiked, please let the UAF researcher know, so they can provide you with a detailed map of that area. On the detailed map, please draw your hiking route as best you can. Please answer the questions on the back of this page that pertain to that unit(s). If you hiked more than approximately ½ mile (0.80 km) away from the road (as shown by the black lines on the map below), answer the questions in this survey only for the conditions you experienced while you were farther than ½ mile (0.80 km) from the road.

Please return the survey to the UAF survey administrator at the Wilderness Access Center, or place the survey in a survey drop box (be sure to fold the detailed route map into the survey). The drop boxes are located at the Wilderness Access Center bus drop-off area and the Backcountry Information Center, by the bear resistant food container drop box.

Thank you for your time. For additional information please contact Dr. Peter Fix, University of Alaska Fairbanks, 907-474-6926, pjfix@alaska.edu.

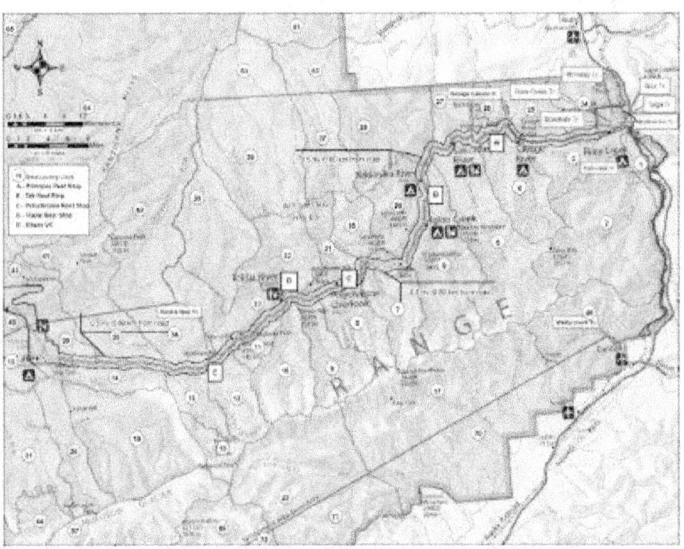

1. **START HERE.** Provide background information regarding your hike or walk.

Backcountry unit(s) you were in _____. *The unit numbers are in the circles, numbered from 1 to 87.*

Today's date: _____. Start time: _____ AM / PM. *Circle one.*

How long did you hike in the backcountry? Please list partial hours as ¼, ½, or ¾. _____ hours.

Did you hike more than ½ mile (0.80 km) into the park? _____ Yes _____ No

Did you hike on an established, maintained trail? _____ Yes _____ No. *This does not include animal trails or social trails.*

How long did you stay on an established trail? Please list partial hours as ¼, ½, or ¾. _____ hours. *This does not include animal trails or social trails.*

Please continue to the back side of this page.

2. While in the backcountry (150 feet (45 meters) from the park road or parking areas), indicate the number of times and the percent of time in which you heard, encountered, or viewed each of the following. *Note: If you hiked more than ½ mile or 0.80 km from the road (see map), please answer these questions only for that portion of time that you were at least ½ mile away from the road.*

A. Motorized sound
     What percent of your time in the backcountry did you hear motorized sound?
     Please check one: ____ 0-24% ____ 25-49% ____ 50-74% ____ 75-100%
	_____ # Encounters

B. Modern equipment
     Includes communication facilities or structures, research equipment, chain saws, and motorized vehicles. Does not include portable devices (GPS units, cell phones), stoves, tents, subsistence equipment, historic buildings/structures, or aircraft.
 	
     What percent of your time in the backcountry was modern equipment visible?
     Please check one: ____ 0-24% ____ 25-49% ____ 50-74% ____ 75-100%
	_____ # Encounters

C. Landscape modifications
     Includes constructed and human-caused trails, route markers, bridges, food storage containers, and the park road. A single trail or route markers associated with one trail count as one encounter. Do not include animal trails.
 	
     What percent of your time in the backcountry were landscape modifications visible?
     Please check one: ____ 0-24% ____ 25-49% ____ 50-74% ____ 75-100%
	_____ # Sightings

D. Park visitors (count groups as one "visitor sighting")
     Unaided (no binoculars or scopes) recognition of other park users, including recreation and subsistence users. This does not include visitors in aircraft.
 	
     What percent of your time in the backcountry were other park visitors visible?
     Please check one: ____ 0-24% ____ 25-49% ____ 50-74% ____ 75-100%
	_____ # Sightings

E. Groups of visitors larger than six	_____ # Encounters
F. National Park Service rangers or researchers *Include interactions with rangers or researchers. Do not include interactions with NPS aircraft or research equipment (include these in the Motorized Sound or Modern Equipment sections, respectively).*	_____ # Encounters
G. Did you have sightings of litter, toilet paper, and/or human waste?	____ Yes ____ No

3. We would like to know whether certain factors negatively impact your backcountry experience. Please indicate if hearing or seeing the following has a negative impact on your experience in the backcountry. (*Circle the most appropriate response.*)

Please rate the impact of hearing or seeing:	No negative impact	Slight negative impact	Moderate negative impact	Significant negative impact
Motorized sound	1	2	3	4
Modern equipment	1	2	3	4
Landscape modifications	1	2	3	4
Park visitors	1	2	3	4
Groups of six or more visitors	1	2	3	4
Toilet paper and human waste	1	2	3	4

Thank you for your time! Please return the survey to a UAF Survey Administrator or to the drop boxes located at the Wilderness Access Center or the Backcountry Information Center.

We are interested in the conditions you experienced during your hike into the backcountry, which is defined as anything ½ mile (0.80 km) or farther from the park road and parking areas. This survey asks about encounters or sightings of certain conditions. The pages repeat as there is a separate page to complete for each backcountry unit you traveled in or each day of your trip.

Complete a separate page for each:
- Unit you traveled in on a given day, or
- The entire day if you only traveled in one unit during that day.

Example: if on day one you traveled through units 8 and 9 and on day two you traveled through unit 9, you would complete separate pages for: unit 8 of day one, unit 9 of day one, and unit 9 of day two.

Use the map below, along with your backcountry permit, to identify the backcountry unit(s) in which you hiked. The backcountry units are the numbers inside the circles. When your hike is complete draw an approximation of your route on the map below. Label campsites sequentially using letters (e.g., A, B, C, etc.).

After your trip, please return the survey to a University of Alaska Fairbanks survey administrator or place the survey in a survey drop box. The drop boxes are located at the Wilderness Access Center bus drop-off area and the Backcountry Information Center, by the bear resistant food container drop box.

Thank you for your time. For additional information please contact Dr. Peter Fix, University of Alaska Fairbanks, 907-474-6926, pjfix@alaska.edu.

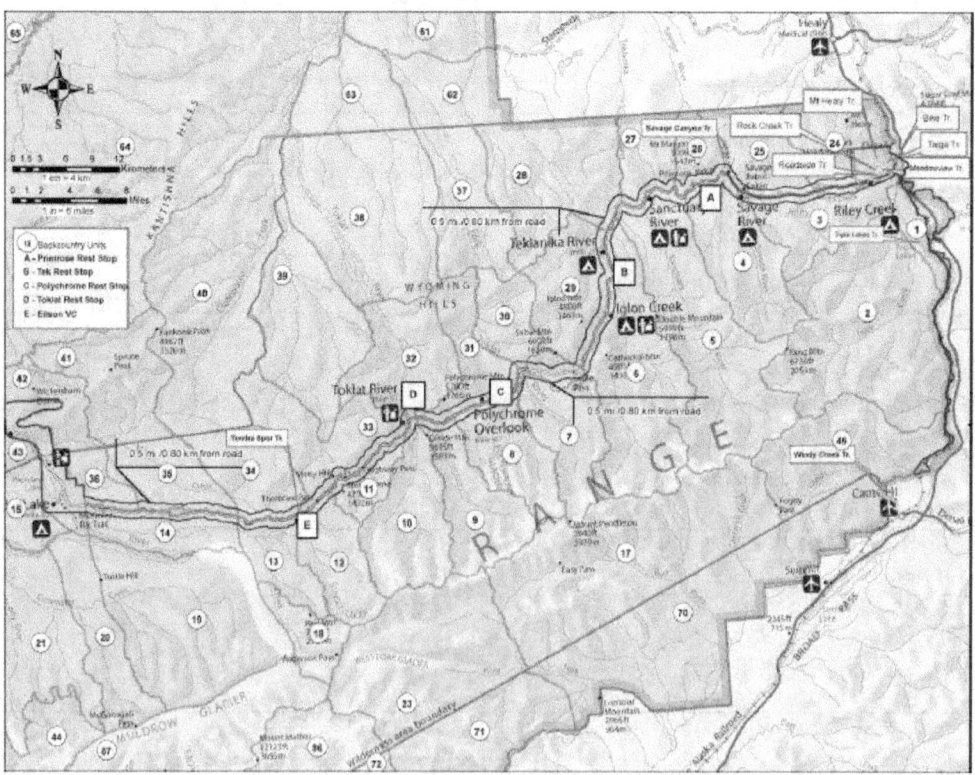

Complete this page for the first day or unit of your hike in the backcountry.

1. Provide background information regarding the first day or unit of your hike. Include the night spent camping in the "day," i.e., the day ends in the a.m.

Backcountry unit you were in: _____. *The unit numbers are in the circles on the map, numbered from 1 to 87.*

Start date: _____. Start time: _____ AM / PM. *Circle one.*

Finish date: _____. Finish time: _____ AM / PM. *Circle one.*

---

2. While in the backcountry (½ mile or farther from the park road or parking areas), indicate the number of times and the percent of time in which you heard, encountered, or viewed each of the following.

A. Motorized sound

    What percent of your time in the backcountry did you hear motorized sound?

    Please check one: _____ 0-24% _____ 25-49% _____ 50-74% _____ 75-100%

_____ # Encounters

B. Modern equipment

    Includes communication facilities or structures, research equipment, chain saws, and motorized vehicles. Does not include portable devices (GPS units, cell phones), stoves, tents, subsistence equipment, historic buildings/structures, or aircraft.

    What percent of your time in the backcountry was modern equipment visible?

    Please check one: _____ 0-24% _____ 25-49% _____ 50-74% _____ 75-100%

_____ # Encounters

C. Landscape modifications

    Includes constructed and human-caused trails, route markers, bridges, food storage containers, and the park road. A single trail or route markers associated with one trail count as one encounter. Do not include animal trails.

    What percent of your time in the backcountry were landscape modifications visible?

    Please check one: _____ 0-24% _____ 25-49% _____ 50-74% _____ 75-100%

_____ # Sightings

D. Park visitors (count groups as one "visitor sighting")

    Unaided (no binoculars or scopes) recognition of other park users, including recreation and subsistence users. This does not include visitors in aircraft.

    What percent of your time in the backcountry were other park visitors visible?

    Please check one: _____ 0-24% _____ 25-49% _____ 50-74% _____ 75-100%

_____ # Sightings

E. Groups of visitors larger than six

_____ # Encounters

F. National Park Service rangers or researchers

    Include interactions with rangers or researchers. Do not include interactions with NPS aircraft or research equipment (include these in the Motorized Sound or Modern Equipment sections, respectively).

_____ # Encounters

G. Did you have sightings of litter, toilet paper, and/or human waste?

_____ Yes _____ No

H. Were you able to camp out of sight and sound of other park visitors?

_____ Yes _____ No

If you are not spending any more days in the backcountry, or visiting other units, go to page 8.

2

113

The previous page repeated on pages 3, 4, 5, 6, and 7. The header was changed to say "second day," "third day," "fourth day," etc.

13. Please draw an approximation of your route on the map on the cover of this survey. Label campsites sequentially with letters (e.g., the first campsite labeled as "A," the second campsite labeled as "B," etc.).

14. We would like to know whether certain factors negatively impact your backcountry experience. Please indicate if hearing or seeing the following has a negative impact on your experience in the backcountry. (*Circle the most appropriate response.*)

Please rate the impact of hearing or seeing:	No negative impact	Slight negative impact	Moderate negative impact	Significant negative impact
Motorized sound	1	2	3	4
Modern equipment	1	2	3	4
Landscape modifications	1	2	3	4
Park visitors	1	2	3	4
Groups of six or more visitors	1	2	3	4
Toilet paper and human waste	1	2	3	4
Others while camping	1	2	3	4

15. Please rate your encounters with National Park Service rangers in the backcountry.

Circle one: Extremely negative   Negative   Average   Positive   Extremely positive   Did not encounter

Please explain your rating in #15:

Are there other factors, not included in this survey, that are important to your backcountry experience in Denali National Park and Preserve?

Thank you for your time! Please return the survey to a UAF survey administrator or place the survey in the survey drop box. The drop boxes are located at the Wilderness Access Center bus drop off area and the Backcountry Information Center, by the bear resistant food container drop box.

Semi-Structured Interview Guide

The Paperwork Reduction Act requires approval of all federal government surveys by the Office of Management and Budget. This survey has been approved under this Act. The Office of Management and Budget control number and expiration date is available at your request. Additional information about this survey and its approval is available at your request.* The questions I would like to ask will only take about **20** minutes to complete. All of your answers are voluntary.

Would it be okay if I recorded this interview? If not, I can take written notes.

1. Could you expand on the ratings of the importance of items A through F? **(Interviewer can read items A-F. Add item G for overnight users.)** In other words, why were some rated as having no negative impact and other rated as having significant negative impact?

1a. **(If all were significant impact)** If you had to rank the items rated, which would you choose as the most important and which as the least important?

1b. **(If some were no negative impact)** Although you feel some are not important, do you think it's still useful for Denali National Park to monitor these items?

2. Are there other factors besides those mentioned that are important to the quality of your experience in the Denali backcountry?

2a. **(If interviewee is not specific on the suggestions)** Could you narrow your suggestion(s) to a factor(s) Denali National Park could monitor?

3. I would like to explore the issue of the impacts of evidence of modern human use on the backcountry experience at Denali National Park.

3a. To what extent did modern human use, or modern civilization, have a positive or negative impact on your backcountry experience during this trip? **(Ask them to elaborate as necessary)**

3b. **(Depending on answer to 3a)** Is it useful for the park to try to monitor impacts of modern human use?

3b.1 **(If yes)** Is monitoring encounters with modern equipment and/or landscape modifications an adequate measure of impacts of modern human use on the backcountry experience?

3c. **(If no to 3b.1)** What would you suggest the park monitor as a measure of the impact of modern human use, or civilization, on the backcountry experience?

3d. **(If yes to 3b.1)** Are there other factors related to the impact of modern human use, or civilization, on the backcountry experience the park should monitor?

*Additional Information Provided upon Request.

OMB Approval number: *(1024-0224(NPS 09-011))*
Expiration Date: *(12/31/2010)*
Person Collecting and Analyzing Information: *(Peter Fix, 323 O'Neill, University of
Alaska Fairbanks, Fairbanks, AK 99775, pjfix@alaska.edu)*

16 U.S.C. 1a-7 authorizes collection of this information. This information will be used by park managers to better serve the public. Response to this request is voluntary. No action may be taken against you for refusing to supply the information requested. No personal data will be recorded.

You may direct comments on the number of minutes required to respond, or on any other aspect of this survey to:
Peter Fix, 323 O'Neill, University of Alaska Fairbanks, Fairbanks, AK 99775, pjfix@alaska.edu

Appendix C. Randomly Selected Sample Dates

BIC = Backcountry Information Center
WAC = Wilderness Access Center
SAV = Savage River

TRI = Triple lakes Trailhead
I = Interview

June

Day	9 am to 1:30 pm	1:30 to 6:30 pm	6:30 to 10:30 pm
1	BIC		WAC
2			WAC
3	BIC		WAC
4			
5			
6		WAC	
7			WAC
8		WAC	WAC
9		BIC/WAC	
10		BIC	
11			
12		BIC/WAC	
13	BIC		WAC
14		BIC	
15			SAV
16			WAC
17		BIC	WAC
18		BIC	WAC
19	BIC	BIC/WAC	
20	BIC	BIC	
21	BIC		WAC
22		BIC	
23	BIC	BIC/WAC/I	WAC
24	BIC		WAC/I
25		BIC	
26		SAV	
27	BIC	BIC	WAC
28	BIC	BIC	
29	BIC		WAC
30		WAC	

July

Day	9 am to 1:30 pm	1:30 to 6:30 pm	6:30 to 10:30 pm
1	BIC	WAC/I	
2		BIC/WAC	
3	BIC		
4		BIC/WAC	WAC
5	BIC		
6		BIC/WAC	
7		WAC/I	
8	BIC		
9	BIC		WAC/I
10		BIC	WAC
11		BIC/WAC	WAC
12			
13		WAC	
14		BIC	
15	BIC		
16	BIC	BIC	
17	BIC	WAC	WAC/I
18			
19	BIC		
20		BIC/WAC	WAC
21	BIC		
22		BIC/WAC	WAC/I
23			
24			
25	BIC	WAC	WAC
26		BIC/WAC	
27	BIC	BIC	WAC
28		BIC/WAC	WAC/I
29			WAC/I
30	BIC	BIC	
31		BIC/WAC/I	WAC

	August		
	Time period to sample		
Day	**9 am to 1:30 pm**	**1:30 to 6:30 pm**	**6:30 to 10:30 pm**
1		BIC/WAC	TRI
2	BIC	BIC	WAC/I
3			
4			
5		BIC	
6	BIC	BIC	TRI
7	BIC	WAC/I	WAC
8	BIC		WAC/I
9	BIC	BIC	TRI
10	BIC		WAC
11		WAC/I	
12		WAC	
13			
14		BIC/WAC	WAC/I
15			
16		WAC	
17		WAC/I	WAC
18	BIC		
19			
20	BIC	WAC	WAC
21			WAC
22		WAC	
23	BIC	SAV	
24			
25	BIC	BIC	WAC/I
26		BIC	WAC
27	BIC	BIC	WAC
28			
29			WAC
30			WAC/I
31		WAC	

	September		
	Time period to sample		
Day	**9 am to 1:30 pm**	**1:30 to 6:30 pm**	**6:30 to 10:30 pm**
1			n/a
2			n/a
3			n/a
4	WAC		n/a
5	WAC		n/a

Appendix D. Comments Written On Backpacker Surveys

Comments have spelling and some grammatical corrections, but otherwise appear as written. For comments with multiple sentences, the section relevant to the theme in which it is grouped is shown in bold font.

Access
Negative
- Access was difficult due to traveling by bike.
- **Getting there (to start the hike) and back is difficult and tedious.** The camper bus broke down and buses are infrequent etc.

Motorized sound
Neutral
- Chose unit 24 as an introduction to Denali 75% of the time was on park trail. So that explains other visitors, trails and motorized sound.

Modern Equipment
Negative
- **Denali is supposed to be wilderness. Construction other than road maintenance negatively affects the experience.** Besides the more structures there are the less it seems like wilderness. The cost of the bus is also a neg. factor. Also Denali is supposed to be trailless

Landscape Modification
Positive
- **Enjoyed Eielson, love the LEED approach to design of the visitor's center.** Bus system seems to work well.
- Thank you for keeping the backcountry trailless and unmodified.

Negative
- The book barn in unit 10 is visible for miles- what I don't like is that we're not supposed to be visible to the tourists when were in the backcountry-but what about what we have to see when we're in the backcountry?
- Denali is supposed to be wilderness. Construction other than road maintenance negatively affects the experience. **Besides the more structures there are the less it seems like wilderness.** The cost of the bus is also a neg. factor. Also Denali is supposed to be trailless

Park Road
Negative
- NPS very helpful, informative and enthusiastic. **Seeing the road from such a far distance away was a distraction from the backcountry experience.**
- Retaining low user numbers per unit. Limiting or not allowing personal traffic (esp. RVs) on the park road. **Having to be out of sight of road even when over three miles away seems unnecessary and limited our campsite choices.**

Planes

<u>Neutral</u>
- All motorized sound was airplanes overhead. Sometimes we could see them-other times not.
- Did not want to do survey for whole trip. **Motorized sound almost entirely aircraft. Seemed dependant on location, weather and by circumstance near rushing water vs. quiet ridgeline.**
- The only motorized sound we heard was airplanes and I don't know that I would have noticed if I hadn't read the survey prior to hiking.

<u>Mixed</u>
- **While the noise from flight seeing planes didn't have a sig. neg. impact on our backcountry experience, it still was fairly noticeable** and if the number of flights increase, it could have the potential to lead to neg. exp. for future backcountry campers/hikers.
- Denali is so incredible that the few interruptions were not a big deal. **The airplanes and helicopter were the most annoying.** But, we encountered no other human signs except along the road and igloo campground. Absolutely no trash of any kind. Very few boot prints.

<u>Negative</u>
- Airplanes make it very difficult to enjoy the backcountry!
- **All motorized sound was airplanes which were annoying** didn't mind buses driving. Saw trails that appeared to be used by people from Eielson appeared to be used more by animals.
- Almost all encounters with modern people and equipment were from small aircraft flying above, **the number of small planes most days seemed excessive**; otherwise it was a very primitive experience.
- Did not encounter NPS this time. When I have they have always been positive and unobtrusive. Less buses less buses, **not only are the planes and helicopters extremely annoying**, but too many buses stalking wildlife on the road is going to leave Denali a sad, empty place. Thanks
- If there is one thing that ruins my backcountry experience it's those awful airplanes and helicopters.
- Overall an excellent experience, but too many other campers. **Low flying small aircraft were annoying.**
- Ran into ranger in unit 10 politely asked to see my permit if it was possible to easily get it out of my bag. **By the end of my hike, the regular sound of air planes flying over started to get annoying.**
- The air traffic can be pretty heavy at times and had the greatest negative impact of anything we encountered.
- The air traffic was pretty heavy at some points and was by far the biggest annoyance.
- Too many planes!
- Two encounters with NPS, they were very pleasant and helpful, checked permits and wished us well, helped with routes and campsite suggestions. **The plane and helicopter exposure was almost nonstop. Airplanes disrupted experience and caribou nearby.**
- I think that human beings are a part of nature. Thus I think it is ok to see traces of them. **It is beneficial to the park experience if flight traffic is limited.** I am from Sweden and thought the park experience was excellent.

Buses
<u>Positive</u>
- **Bus drivers rock!** Need more outbound buses mid afternoon.
- Enjoyed Eielson, love the LEED approach to design of the visitor's center. **Bus system seems to work well.**

<u>Neutral</u>
- All motorized sound was airplanes which were annoying **didn't mind buses driving.** Saw trails that appeared to be used by people from Eielson appeared to be used more by animals.

<u>Negative</u>
- Car seats for infants- 4 yrs is a major obstacle to family backpacking. The bus system is way overpriced and doesn't have enough shuttles to make it a reliable mode of transportation. Free shuttles leaving savage every two hours? Ridiculous.
- Denali is supposed to be wilderness. Construction other than road maintenance negatively affects the experience. Besides the more structures there are the less it seems like wilderness. **The cost of the bus is also a neg. factor.** Also Denali is supposed to be trailless.
- Did not encounter NPS this time. When I have they have always been positive and unobtrusive. **Less buses less buses, not only are the planes and helicopters extremely annoying, but too many buses stalking wildlife on the road is going to leave Denali a sad, empty place.** Thanks
- Getting there (to start the hike) and back is difficult and tedious. The camper bus broke down and buses are infrequent etc.

<u>Suggestions</u>
- Bus drivers rock! **Need more outbound buses mid afternoon.**
- Didn't encounter NPS/ **need more signage showing pick up locations camper bus.**
- **More morning BC buses to insure that not all buses are full for campers trying to get an early departure.**

Trails
<u>Positive</u>
- Seeing animals in their home was very valuable to my experience. **Not having trails was also important**. [*negative towards trails; positive towards no trails*]. The rangers' passion for the part was also a positive experience for us.

- **Thank you for keeping the backcountry trailless and unmodified.** [*negative towards trails; but positive toward the current situation in the park*]

<u>Neutral</u>
- All motorized sound was airplanes which were annoying didn't mind buses driving. **Saw trails that appeared to be used by people from Eielson appeared to be used more by animals.**
- **Chose unit 24 as an introduction to Denali 75% of the time was on park trail. So that explains other visitors, trails** and motorized sound.

121

- Denali is supposed to be wilderness. Construction other than road maintenance negatively affects the experience. Besides the more structures there are the less it seems like wilderness. The cost of the bus is also a neg. factor. **Also Denali is supposed to be trailless.**

Rangers/BIC/Info
Positive
- **Almost all rangers here are amazing**. One didn't know the rules on how far to camp from the road.
- Backcountry office very helpful and patient, willing to help accommodate our larger (6) group as able.
- **BIC rangers friendly and helpful**. Animal sights and vegetation terrace encounters.
- **Did not encounter NPS this time. When I have they have always been positive and unobtrusive**. Less buses less buses, not only are the planes and helicopters extremely annoying, but too many buses stalking wildlife on the road is going to leave Denali a sad, empty place. Thanks
- Knowledgeable people at NPS to give valid info on hiking backcountry.
- No encounters in backcountry with rangers but extremely helpful info in BIC.
- NPS extremely friendly and helpful.
- **NPS gave correct and adequate info, nice people.** Woken by wolves growling and investigating food containers. They should be white and lighter instead of black and rather heavy.
- NPS rangers at Eielson visitor center were knowledgeable helpful and courteous.
- NPS very friendly, informative and helpful.
- **NPS very helpful, informative and enthusiastic.** Seeing the road from such a far distance away was a distraction from the backcountry experience.
- NPS was inquisitive, happy to see us and very informative with regards to our continued journey.
- **NPS was nice and pointed out a bear and two cubs she had seen earlier for our awareness.** We were far away though and the bears had wandered off before we got there. It left us a bit apprehensive since we didn't know where they went.
- Pre backcountry education was superb to ensure the possibility of a true backcountry experience.
- Rangers encountered were great, but not seen in backcountry. Did an MSLC course as well-excellent.
- Seeing animals in their home was very valuable to my experience. Not having trails was also important. **The rangers' passion for the part was also a positive experience for us.**
- The backcountry center rangers and Eielson rangers were very helpful.
- The guys at the WAC were incredible. Thank you guys, it was wonderful!
- **Two encounters with NPS, they were very pleasant and helpful, checked permits and wished us well, helped with routes and campsite suggestions.** The plane and helicopter exposure was almost nonstop. Airplanes disrupted experience and caribou nearby.
- Very helpful at backcountry permit bldg.
- WAC/BIC people were friendly and gave helpful advice.
- We really appreciated the advise and the safety info and the rangers helping us plan a trip

<u>Neutral</u>
- **Didn't encounter NPS/** need more signage showing pick up locations camper bus
- Only saw NPS Ranger at designated spots on road centers.
- Park service was working at Toklat. Road research I think.
- **Ran into ranger in unit 10 politely asked to see my permit if it was possible to easily get it out of my bag.** By the end of my hike, the regular sound of air planes flying over started to get annoying.
- The positive interactions I have had with the Rangers at the backcountry office have had a significant impact on my experience in preparing to go out into the backcountry and is also a part of enjoying Denali backcountry.
- **The ranger (Julie) at the Toklat station was very helpful in giving route recommendations.** /wild life sightings add to backcountry experience.
- We didn't encounter any rangers during our backcountry experience. So, as a consequence, we voted to circle "did not encounter."

<u>Negative</u>
- Almost all rangers here are amazing. **One didn't know the rules on how far to camp from the road.**
- I would like to get better info about the area I'm going to hike. Area 34 is not nice to hike we didn't know that and nobody told us.
- May have been told that after arriving at backcountry permit office for info that first we could take out to set off, was at 1400 1100am was too short notice for us.
- Presence of private prop signs need to be explained better to visitors. **Were told two different things about what to do with private prop signs.**
- The park ranger was leading a group of ten or so hikers and he brought the group right up to where we were. He didn't even try to avoid us. We had to wait awhile for them to pass in order to cont. on and enjoy our time
- The rangers in the backcountry office neglected to give us a portion of the map we needed for our unit. This made it very difficult once we were out there. We did not know this had happened until it was too late.
- When leaving into savage creek drainage, Ranger at the station was not as helpful as he could have been (limited info offered).
- Would have liked more advice on terrain from BIC. Info on crossing choke points like Muldrow and McKinley River would be useful. We were unable to find a crossing point during the time we had.
- Would have liked to receive more descriptive intro to camping zones in the unit. The info and pictures in the backcountry office do not provide enough guidance for hikers who will only be able to visit each unit once and for a short period of time.

<u>Suggestions</u>
- During inclement weather it would be good to have someone checking sectors for passability etc. Got stuck by a river on the last day. A warning system for hard to reach or unsafe areas should be in place.
- It would be beneficial to have an idea of places able for camping in each zone would be very beneficial.

- Limited access is great but 1 day makes planning difficult-would prefer at least some areas were "reservable" a few days-2 weeks in advance so that trail maps/supplies, etc can be gathered in advance lockers at WAC were very helpful for stashing unneeded equipment.
- Longer hours for backcountry permit desk with more staff.
- **Presence of private prop signs need to be explained better to visitors.** Were told two different things about what to do with private prop signs.

Other Visitors
Positive
- **I think that human beings are a part of nature. Thus I think it is ok to see traces of them.** It is beneficial to the park experience if flight traffic is limited. I am from Sweden and thought the park experience was excellent.
- The quotas (or hikers in each region) and the resulting low numbers of encounters with other hikers contributed significantly and positively to our backcountry experience.

Neutral
- **Chose unit 24 as an introduction to Denali 75% of the time was on park trail. So that explains other visitors**, Trails and motorized sound.
- **I think that human beings are a part of nature. Thus I think it is ok to see traces of them**. It is beneficial to the park experience if flight traffic is limited. [*negative toward heavy use? positive towards limiting user numbers*] I am from Sweden and thought the park experience was excellent.
- Only saw one researcher, no interaction.
- The airplanes and helicopter were the most annoying. **But, we encountered no other human signs except along the road and igloo campground.** Absolutely no trash of any kind. Very few boot prints.
- **Man camping in what appeared to be the day use area before unit 14. I didn't see a permit on his tent but he had a bear can**. Saw a caribou by the river and it was lovely. :)

Negative
- Overall an excellent experience, but **too many other campers**. Low flying small aircraft were annoying.
- The park ranger was leading a group of ten or so hikers and he brought the group right up to where we were. He didn't even try to avoid us. We had to wait awhile for them to pass in order to cont. on and enjoy our time.

Suggestions
- **Retaining low user numbers per unit.** Limiting or not allowing personal traffic (esp. RVs) on the park road. Having to be out of sight of road even when over three miles away seems unnecessary and limited our campsite choices.

Camp out of Sight/Sound
Neutral
- Wildlife viewing important. **Other campers set up camp visible from where we were**. Had a great time watching a large grizzly.

Litter/Human Waste
Neutral
- Saw a pile of building refuse on the gravel head of the confluence of the East and West fork of Glenn Creek.
- The airplanes and helicopter were the most annoying. But, we encountered no other human signs except along the road and igloo campground. **Absolutely no trash of any kind.** Very few boot prints.

Other Things
Positive
- **Seeing animals in their home was very valuable to my experience**. Not having trails was also important. The rangers' passion for the part was also a positive experience for us.
- The magnitude of Denali significantly adds extreme beneficial way to my backcountry experience. Federal protection and preservation adds to my experience it gives it a sense of timeless immaculatuity (immaculate and perpetuity).
- The planning and education the NPS uses to help protect the wilderness of Denali I value the purposeful effect by the NPS to protect the wilderness experience and the ecosystem. While nothing is perfect I appreciate the effort and cont. attempt to revise the management for the best.
- The ranger (Julie) at the Toklat station was very helpful in giving route recommendations. **Wild life sightings add to backcountry experience.**
- **Wildlife viewing important.** Other campers set up camp visible from where we were. Had a great time watching a large grizzly.

Negative
- **The new law that allows loaded firearms into the park (wilderness).** Please push to have this law changed. This is a tranquil and scenic place and loaded weapons do not belong here...
- The weather got foggy and couldn't see anything, I took a short walk to check any visibility and match the map then got lost, I'm having a hard time to go back to my tent.

Suggestions
- The new law that allows loaded firearms into the park (wilderness). **Please push to have this law changed. This is a tranquil and scenic place and loaded weapons do not belong here...**

Modern Human Use
Neutral
- **I think that human beings are a part of nature. Thus I think it is ok to see traces of them.** It is beneficial to the park experience if flight traffic is limited. I am from Sweden and thought the park experience was excellent.
- I am a park employee and hold the idea of Denali and its wildness close to my heart. Therefore I have a jaded understanding and appreciation of the park, infrastructure and its maintenance needs. Also did not camp far from the road.

General
<u>Positive</u>
- Great trip
- I think you got it covered :).
- It was amazing.
- It was beautiful!
- It was everything we wanted.
- It's so beautiful, let us all cont. preserving and protecting amazing wilderness like this forever.
- Man camping in what appeared to be the day use area before unit 14. I didn't see a permit on his tent but he had a bear can. **Saw a caribou by the river and it was lovely. :)**
- No we had a wonderful experience.
- We had an awesome experience.

<u>Neutral</u>
- In three days I only saw one fox and a few birds, this is not the parks fault.
- **Man camping in what appeared to be the day use area before unit 14. I didn't see a permit on his tent but he had a bear can.** Saw a caribou by the river and it was lovely. :)

<u>Negative</u>
- **Lots of mosquitoes and lots of rain.** Better rain gear would have been helpful, mosquito net is a necessity!

<u>Suggestions</u>
- Need more fish
- NPS gave correct and adequate info, nice people. Woken by wolves growling and investigating **food containers. They should be white and lighter instead of black and rather heavy.**

NPS 184/109205, August 2011